What People Are Saying about

WALKING THROUGH YOUR WALLS

"I absolutely love this book! It's filled with content and helpful information."

— Dr. Bertha Barraza, Author of *Completing a College Degree*

"You should really read this book; I learned *so* much about life from it."

— Ping Nip, Author of *Behind the Door*

"I am already making great improvements in my life, and I'm only a little way through it! It's great!"

— Laurie Bethell Bratt, Author of *Bear Witness*

"Lynda Lamp is such a great writer that you'll feel as if she is speaking directly to you, sitting there with you, holding your hand, even."

— Mikki Wade, Author of *Rediscovering Your Authentic Self*

"You will be blown away by what you will learn here!"

— Jeffrey A. Barnes, Author of *The Wisdom of Walt: Leadership Lessons from the Happiest Place on Earth*

"This is the book you've been looking for; I don't know anyone who doesn't just love it!"

— Kevin A. Dunlap, Author of *Designing Your Own Destiny*

"The world is waking up, and this book has come at the perfect time! You'll be so happy you made the investment—get the printed copy. You're going to want this book in your library forever."

— Renee Merlo, Author of *Design & Sewing Trade Secrets*

"You're never too old to give up ways of being that don't serve you. Do yourself a favor; read this book."

— Susan Ortolano, Author of *Remarrying Right*

"I am so excited by the things I've read in this book. I can see the world in such a different way now. I'm learning what's really mine to deal with; it's making a huge difference in my life."

— Jim W. Connolly, Author of *Creating Leaders to Build Teams*

"There's so much about our daily lives that I bet you never even think about, right? I know I didn't. Lynda Lamp brings it all out in a really accessible way. It'll blow your mind! In a good way!"

— Renee Michelle Gordon, Author of
Finding Your Love At Last

"I've read so many books looking for answers, and here are all the answers you need, in a brilliant presentation."

— Karina Tangwalder, Author of
Climbing Your Route to Success

HUMANITY'S HANDBOOK TO LIVING CONSCIOUSLY IN THE TWENTY-FIRST CENTURY

WALKING THROUGH YOUR WALLS

LOVING YOURSELF (AND EVERYONE ELSE)

VOLUME I

LYNDA LAMP

AVIVA PUBLISHING
New York

Walking Through Your Walls: Loving Yourself and Everyone Else, Volume I

Address all inquiries to:

Lynda Lamp
P.O. Box 1741
13725 Beach Drive, Lowell Point
Seward, AK 99664-1741
1-(855) 763-LOVE (5683)
LyndaLamp@LyndaLamp.com
www.LyndaLamp.com

ISBN: 978-1-9431646-6-0
Library of Congress #: 2016943165

Editors: Tyler Tichelaar and Larry Alexander, Superior Book Productions
Cover and Interior Design: Angel Dog Productions

Published by:
Aviva Publishing
Lake Placid, NY
1- (518) 523-1320
www.avivapubs.com

Every attempt has been made to source properly all quotes.

Printed in the USA

First Edition

For additional copies visit:
www.LyndaLamp.com
www.WalkingThroughYourWalls.com

DEDICATION

This book is dedicated to you, my reader, that you may find your true way in this third-dimensional realm to the power of the Universe within you, that you become all that you dream of in the core of your being—the dreams you don't share with anyone because they seem too big, too impossible, too beyond your reach. Nothing is beyond your reach; as long as your dreams resonate with the good of the whole, and you desire to be the best you can become, there's nothing you can't do. This book is dedicated to you and your pursuit of your dreams.

On a personal note, this book is dedicated to my grandchildren, and all the children of the world. May you find this handbook useful.

ACKNOWLEDGMENTS

This book has been made possible by every single human being who has ever crossed my path. From my mother, where I started, to the doctor who cut her open to rescue me, to the very last person I've interacted with—every single person, every single moment, and everything in between has led me to the penning of this acknowledgment. Whether you are someone I see every day, or you're one of the many people who may think, "I knew this woman once," I acknowledge and thank you!

I love you all, and I love the contribution you have made in my becoming. The one person I will acknowledge by name is my beloved husband, Paul, who indeed is my spirit mate, the person I searched for from day one, the person I was meant to find, and the person who has provided me the nurturing and loving environment that has allowed me to evolve. He totally supports my life mission and joins me in sharing the beautiful splendor of life with as much of humanity as we can reach, either through our small lodging business or through these books and my speaking and coaching. For the role each of you has played, I acknowledge and thank you from the depth of my spirit. Namaste.

My favorite translation of Namaste: I honor the place in you which is of love, light, peace, and joy. When you are in that place in you, and I am in that place in me, we are one.

CONTENTS

Appendices

A SPECIAL INVITATION

A Special Invitation to You, My Beloved Reader:

I am here to support you in your quest for knowledge and understanding of how to live consciously in the twenty-first century. Making changes can feel like a daunting task, but you are not alone or without help! I am here, and I will connect you with other like-minded people. We are all in this together. This is a book series unlike any other. I intend to take advantage of technology and keep these books as current as possible. As I issue updates, you'll receive notices and the updates themselves! I would be humbled and honored if you would opt in to my mailing list. To do so, please visit: WalkingThroughYourWalls.com and sign up.

You'll receive notifications about updates to this book, newly released videos, discussion groups, and more. I am also available for workshops, speaking events, and counseling sessions (long distance and in person), and I will be continually releasing free training videos and other resource materials. My author website is: LyndaLamp.com. Please visit the book's Facebook page and join the conversation! Feel free to post your comments, questions, and thoughts as you read this book. Just go to: https://www.facebook.com/WalkingThroughYourWalls

I look forward to hearing from you and walking with you through your walls!

Namaste,

Lynda Lamp

Lynda Lamp

OVERVIEW OF THIS HANDBOOK

Due to the size of this handbook, it has been broken down into multiple volumes. Although they are intended to be read in order, each volume can also stand on its own.

Here is a brief overview of the current volumes (subject to change).

Volume I: Walking Through Your Walls ~ From One Wall to Another

Section 1: The Halls of History

Section 2: The Walls of Life

Volume I lays the foundations for a shift in consciousness. This volume is a great starting place if you are new to the idea that there is something more going on here in the third dimension. This volume contains introductory exercises in presence and mindfulness; it starts a review of your chakra energy system, and there is a supplement with seven tools to get you started in walking through your walls.

Volume II: Walking Through Your Walls ~ From Walls to Windows

Section 3: The Tools of Life

Section 4: The Way to Love

Volume II details the tools available to you for making the shift in consciousness and awakening. It gives practical examples of the application of the tools in the arenas of self-love and love of others. This volume is the core of the handbook and should become an invaluable book in your library.

Volume III: Walking Through Your Walls ~ From Windows to Doors

Section 5: The Way to Health

Section 6: Walking a New Walk

Section 7: Making a New World

Volume III contains the sections of the handbook that give you new systems and structures to employ to create the new world we all want—starting first with our health, then a world of peace, harmony, and love. Volume III is ideal for more advanced spirits who are experienced in the practice of presence and oneness and are ready to start walking their light out into the world, spreading the message of *unconditional, infinite love, and oneness* through the practice of mindfulness and consciousness.

Volume III starts with the fundamentals of getting healthy and becoming a model of the principles of self-love and infinite love of others; for until you have that love, true health will elude you.

Volume III provides several new systems or structures you can employ to create tangible change in your external world: ANGELS Care Inc., Love By LIGHT, and WE LOVE US.

The sections of the handbook correlate to the Human Energetic Chakra system. If you are familiar with the chakras, they will be meaningful. If you are not familiar with the chakra system, no worries! You'll learn as we go along together.

It is my hope that everyone will find something of value in each volume, but feel free to start with the volume that resonates best with your studies and experience.

"Blessed are the cracked, for they shall let in the light."

— Groucho Marx

PREFACE

"The important thing is not to stop questioning. Curiosity has its own reason for existing. One cannot help but be in awe when he contemplates the mysteries of eternity, of life, of the marvelous structure of reality. It is enough if one tries merely to comprehend a little of this mystery every day. Never lose a holy curiosity."

— Albert Einstein

You need a manual to life—we all do, don't we? Some kind of "operator's manual" or "handbook." Douglas Adams gave us *A Hitchhiker's Guide to the Universe*, but, seriously, wouldn't it be helpful to have a real handbook?

That's what this three-volume series is. Humanity's handbook for living consciously. This book is for you. Every...single...one... of...you! As such, it is written a certain way so it can be relatable to everyone. That I have found to be a bit of a challenge!

We must find some common ground to stand upon while we take the questions and study of creation and life in this physical three-dimensional reality deeper and further than ever before.

I go into the following concepts in greater detail in the chapter titled "Deconstructing Religion," but for just a moment, I want to cover a few changes in language that I'll be using throughout this book.

What I am asking you to do is to be open minded; please do not judge me or these words, but allow them just to be. Allow your body and heart to sit with them instead of allowing your mind to rush to judgment. Some of what I suggest may not be easy to accept at first. Don't worry about memorizing the list below. As each term comes up in the handbook, I'll review the term again.

It is my hope that as you get to know me through these writings, you'll come to feel and believe that I have only your best and greatest interests at heart, and that you will come to know that I am one of the most religious and spiritual people you may ever meet. I hope to show you what it truly means to embody the messages the ascended masters teach.

In this book, I will use the following terms:

♥ **AAH** and the **All That IS**, in place of the word "God." This will also replace references to "The Void." (There is no void, but I reference it because others believe in it.) We'll go into AAH in great detail in Volume I, Chapter 6, Deconstructing Religion. Briefly, AAH is the sound most of the traditional words for God make, in addition to playing on the sound of an "Ahh Ha moment." While spelled differently, the sound is basically the same.

- ♥ **Parent, Our Parent, Our Shared Parent, or Great Parent, also Great One Mind** in place of references to Father, or The Father, or Holy Father.
- ♥ **Yeshua Ben Joseph** for Jesus (the man).
- ♥ **Oneness** for all references to Christ.
- ♥ **ISness, All That IS, and Oneness Consciousness**, for references to Christ Consciousness, or Conquering Christ, or any similar term that implies the "that of God" in each of us.
- ♥ **Soul**, as I use it, means your collective memory of your spirit in this life, and all the other life you have (or lives you have). (If you are wondering why this is in present tense, we'll deal with that in Section 2.)
- ♥ **Spirit**, as I use it, means your energy that is You in *this* life's incarnation in the third dimension.
- ♥ **Universe**, as I use it, means all the "physical matter" that is, which is filled with the essence of AAH and All That IS.
- ♥ **Source**, as I use it, means AAH, the Void (although as stated, this is not a concept I embrace), All That IS, or Great One Mind.
- ♥ **Heavenly, Celestial, or Eternal Life** are words I will use in place of Divinity.

(I will explain all of these later in detail. For now, please just suspend judgment and go with the flow.)

If we are going to learn things together, one of the things we need to do in this handbook is use words that can work (hopefully even in translation) to equalize language into something we can all relate to. Common ground is important; we are all one, so we need to find ways to communicate that transcend tradition.

Thank you in advance for hanging in here!

"Live as if you were to die tomorrow.
Learn as if you were to live forever."

— Mahatma Gandhi

The sections in this book (spread across three volumes) correlate to the human chakra energy system. At the end of some of the chapters within each section, there will be information about the chakras. You'll be given a high level overview of this energy system and some tools to keep your energy centers clear.

There are many philosophies about the chakra system dating back to ancient times. By the time you've completed all seven sections, you'll have a rudimentary understanding of your chakra system.

If you are already familiar with the chakra system, you may still find some interesting information—at a minimum, you'll have a refresher. The clearing statements can be helpful to anyone.

A final note: You may want to have a pen and small notebook available as you are reading. There are some exercises in the handbook, and you may want to make further note of your thoughts and feelings, or questions you'd like to ask me.

"And remember, no matter where you go, there you are."

— Confucius

INTRODUCTION

"The best moments in reading are when you come across something—a thought, a feeling, a way of looking at things—which you had thought special and particular to you. Now here it is, set down by someone else, a person you have never met.... And it is as if a hand has come out and taken yours."

— Alan Bennett

Oh, how I hope those will be our hands joining as these words speak to you!

Thank you! Thank you so much for however you came to be holding this book in your hands and reading this introduction! The book is honored; I am humbled and honored beyond words! This book can feel your hands cradling it. It truly loves the feel of your hands upon it, for it is a book, and it is meant to be held. It wants you to get great value from its pages; it yearns to be a book you will treasure. The ink of these words can feel your eyes upon it and yearns for you to treasure the words it reveals, as do the paper pages.

I was given the gift of sight—not eyesight, although I do have that—but I also have an ability to see things beyond appearances. Some might say I can see the systems at work. Others might say I have deep insight, or that I'm psychic, or clairvoyant, or a channel. I'm all of those things and more; I actually gave up trying to describe it many years ago. It's too strange and convoluted, and it seems no one ever truly understands it—sometimes not even me. A coach I worked with once named me a universe whisperer; it fit so well that it became the name of my life-coaching business.

Lately, though, it seems that there is an "army" of light workers, healers, life coaches, peace makers, love spreaders—suddenly, I'm no longer the oddball, but one of the herd. It feels a whole lot easier to stick my neck out with an idea. Now I can stand in front of a room full of people and talk about how everything is an illusion and not get laughed off the stage. I can say to you, "There's no such thing as time," and instead of your eyes glazing over, you nod, because even if you don't understand how it works, you've heard the saying before.

I was given my sight so that I may share it with you in the form of help, so that you might also come to "see."

"We are all just walking each other home."

— Rumi

In the years prior to finally sitting down to write this book (it's been on my to-do list for over twenty years), I took a number of classes and workshops, and I worked with several life coaches. The question that came up every time, from each teacher or coach, was "Who is your 'tribe'? You need to market to your tribe." My answer is always the same: "Humanity is my tribe! Everyone is part of my tribe!" I can honestly say that no one understood. "You have to have a niche," I was told. They insisted.

To that I say a resounding "No!" We are all one; that is my whole point! Every niche is a separation from the whole. I am speaking to the whole because we are all one. I know this from my personal experience, so no one can, or ever will, convince me differently. You see, life isn't "what we know"; it's what we experience. It is our experiences that give us our true knowledge.

Lately, there's a meme that is going around Facebook: "The Universe is my Home, all beings are my tribe, and Oneness is my religion." This is the point I have always tried to make, but only during the past few years have people seemed to be more open to these ideas.

You are an amazing being. Yes, you, the person holding this book; you are so powerful and so magnificent, capable of anything you set the good of your heart, mind, and energies to. You may not see that, but I do. I see you for all that you are; I see you are limitless.

I so hope the words on these pages speak to your heart. I would love to meet you; I wish we could sit together over a cup of tea or coffee and talk; I know we would have wonderful conversations. I have never met anyone I didn't love learning about. I wish I could learn all about you, so I could personally point you to the volume, sections, or chapters of this book series that will mean the most or be of the most interest to you.

I hope you have already taken time to read the "Overview of This Handbook," which will help you know what each volume contains. If not, you can go back and read it before proceeding to Chapter 1. Although I would be honored if you read all three volumes, it is not necessary. Feel free to jump to the volume that speaks to you. If, however, you find you are having difficulty with implementing systems or achieving goals, you may find you need to go to an earlier volume for some missing foundational work.

Each section in this handbook correlates to one of the chakras in the human energetic body. As you go through the volumes and sections, I will be giving you exercises to clear each of your seven energy centers.

Each of you will come to this handbook with your own unique perspective, personal development level, and knowledge base. The challenge for me has been to put this together in such a way that each of you will find what you need.

"We cannot teach people anything,
we can only help them discover it within themselves."

— Galileo

I am not here to teach you anything; I am here to help you find the answers you seek. You don't realize it, but everything you need, you already have. It is within you. I am here to help you find your true self within, and to bring your truth out so we can all enjoy the special and brilliant you that you are.

This handbook for humanity is the beginning of a worldwide conversation about the systems we can put in practice to bring you and everyone to a new place of understanding, peace, and harmony.

Through this handbook, you will be given a way not only to learn, but a way to share. A truly great handbook is one that is constantly updated with new information. Through the website and Facebook page for this series, we'll build a community and share updates to the handbook, so even if you have a first edition, as further editions are released, you'll have access to all new information.

I also intend your experience to be an interactive one as you are reading these volumes. If you have questions, I invite you to post on the Facebook page, email me at Questions@WalkingThroughYourWalls.com, or call me at 1-(855) 763-LOVE (5683).

Together, we'll build a network—not just online, but in person. Using the systems introduced in these volumes, you'll be equipped to change the world through acts of love, peace, and harmony. If a neighbor or family member needs help, you'll be able to start your own ANGELS Care, Inc. and get things taken care of. You'll be able to start your own heart circle using the model of Love By LIGHT, or you'll be able to find one to attend. You'll use WE LOVE US as daily guidance, and people will wear WE LOVE US wristbands, and businesses will display the WE LOVE US decals in their windows. Finding like-minded people to share community and do business with will be easy.

These systems are covered in depth in Volume III, but you are welcome to visit the websites or Facebook Pages/Groups now for more information, or you may email or call me. There is no reason to wait. See the handbook websites listing in Appendix D for the URLs.

Walking Through Your Walls is a serious sounding title, but we are going to have fun together!

Although at the moment the title is figurative, it is my firm belief that someday you and I will be literally walking through walls—yes, physical walls. We'll talk about this in depth in Section 2 of Volume I. If you are already able to walk through walls, please let me know!

The walls we'll walk through together in this handbook are all the walls that keep you from seeing what is really going on in life. Once you've walked through the walls, you'll find love—love for yourself, because you have to love yourself before you can offer your love to others.

I am here to play the role of the lamp, shining the light on the road you are on; I am here to light the way. Our Shared Parent is laughing that the girl who sees in the darkness and who came here to shine a light on the truth has the initials L.A.M.P. That's a story I'll save for another time. It is not significant to the handbook, but it is a great story.

Picture yourself driving down a country road at night. You can only see as far as your headlights illuminate and just a tad of what you are passing—just what the light of your headlights illuminates around you. You don't stop because you can't see. Even though you can't see more than a few hundred feet ahead of you, you are comfortable barreling down the road, going 45 mph, or 55, or more. That takes faith.

Life is a bit like traveling down that dark country road. You really don't know where you are headed; you really can't see where you are going; you can't even see what you're passing by, but off you go anyway. Life takes faith. And quite often, we find we have more faith in driving down that dark country road than we do in getting up in the morning. Sometimes, life is hard to have faith in.

Now, imagine I'm riding along with you and I have a huge flashlight. With my light, you can see not only where you are going, and what you're passing all round, and where you've been, but you can also really see where you are.

You will no longer be blind to anything; I'm going to take you into the trees, and you will see the forest, and somewhere along the way, you're going to realize that I'm not shining a light, not in front of you, not around you; I'm not shining anything. You are the light, and in that moment, you will see what I see. You will see the forest; you will see the trees; you will see the connections; you will see through the walls to your inner truth.

That's my role here. I am part of what Dianne Collins, in her book *Quantum Think*, calls "wisdom distribution channels."

This handbook is an undertaking of revelation. Through the distribution of universal wisdom, you are going to find help here. Some questions of yours will be answered; some mysteries will be explained. If there is any tiny part of you that is not happy, here is help to find your light within, to allow your happiness to flow. If you are not living your life to your spirit's highest possible expression, here is the support you need to flourish to your finest. If you are ready to start shining your light into the world, moving the message of oneness and mindfulness to others, but you don't know where to start, there is help here for you! If all of these ideas are completely new to you, but you are curious, here is a light along the way for you to begin your exploration. I will help you find those white rocks marking the way home, just like you were Hansel or Gretel.

Whatever challenge you may be experiencing, here is help to overcome it; wherever you are in your life and wherever you dream of going, here is help to achieve your desires.

I honor you as you are, in whatever physical form you have taken, and in whatever mindset you bring to this reading. In these volumes, I am inviting you to come into a new knowingness—a knowingness that comes not from me, but from within you. Not from the voice(s) in your head, or from what those around you tell you, but from your core being, from your soul, your spirit. I am inviting you to understand, once and for all, how life is really working here, on this planet we call Earth, in this physical reality that we call the third dimension. I am inviting you to become the true you.

This handbook is here to help you open up to yourself. It's about you discovering your spirit's fullest potential. It's about you loving yourself beyond anything you have considered—at a depth and breadth that, when you allow your love to flow through you, connects you to every other being on this planet; it connects you to everything animate and inanimate. In that state, everything—the Universe and beyond—feels your love, and love will come rushing back to you tenfold. It is also how you will change the world.

You are an amazing, out of this world, fantastic, powerful, celestial light being, made of the universe and infinitely powerful, with the gifts of all creation at your fingertips just for the asking, for the good of the whole.

Few of you will resonate with that description right now, but I challenge you to stay with me—to finish this handbook, to work your way through the volumes, and then to read this introduction again—then see whether you arrive in a moment of agreement, and marvel with me!

We, humanity, are currently surrounded with negativity and fear, gloom and doom, hate and loathing in our physical world. For many, it is hard to feel hopeful. The world I see, and feel emerging, is a world that embraces the oneness and nowness messages of this handbook. The book market is flooded with self-help, health and healing, enlightenment and light work, and change and leadership books. There are many, many, many books and authors out there who are of great value. What makes this handbook different is that it gathers up all the salient points from start to finish, with exercises, solutions, and systems that can be implemented. Life from start to finish. One thing I see is that all the necessary information is out there in the world, but it's too spread out, it's fractured, so this is an attempt to gather things into one place, into a handbook. I am known to many as "The Great Organizer."

My ability to see patterns has revealed to me a connection between what's going on now, in terms of the movement of oneness and peace, and what went on in the 1960s. There was a huge love and peace, anti-war movement going on in the 1960s. What happened? What happened is that these are lovely notions, but until we change the way we think, until we change the way we behave, until we change ourselves, peace will elude us.

While it appears that the peace and love movement is getting a revival with more and more organizations forming, there are almost two thousand terrorist and antigovernment organizations in the United States alone, and those numbers are also on the rise. Humanity's dream of global peace lives on in the hearts of many, but the disillusionment of hate (the result of fear) lives in many too.

In the meantime, we have evolved as a species; we are capable of so much more than we realize. You are capable of more than you ever used to be. This handbook gives you what the 1960s never did; it gives you a plan; it gives you structures to work with.

It's *not* too late to make changes and to "save" the planet! To say, "It's too late," or "We have to act soon," or "fast" is to declare ourselves without hope, and all that surrounds us hears our lack of faith and responds accordingly. This handbook gives you straightforward formulas, systems, and simple directions to make astounding changes in your world in the areas of peace, love, and joy. "The next Buddha is a Sangha" is a saying in the oneness community, which means that the way to enlightenment will be as a community. It will be a community of Gaia, of infinite, unconditional love, of oneness.

Hold the knowingness that everything is absolutely perfect and unfolding exactly as intended by the Great One Mind. You are here to play your part. Don't worry about what other people are doing; other people are not your business. You are your business; keep your attention on yourself in the now, and ensure that you are being the greatest you whom you can be.

This handbook will show you the way to loving yourself, and loving everyone else. Armed with the formulas and structures of WE LOVE US, Love by LIGHT, and ANGELS Care, you'll easily be able to bring the callings of oneness, infinite love, and forgiveness to your daily life.

While you and I can't walk through physical walls yet, wouldn't you like to go through your days in a state of joy, bursting at the seams with happiness all the time?

You can live a life of bliss once you understand what's going on around you. I promise you that.

Let's begin this journey of exploration (Volume I), discovery (Volume II), and creation (Volume III) together, shall we?

"I expect to pass through this world but once. Any good therefore that I can do, or any kindness that I can show to any fellow creature, let me do it now. Let me not defer nor neglect it for I shall not pass this way again."

— Stephen Grellet

SECTION 1

THE HALLS OF HISTORY

"History is a set of lies agreed upon."

— Napoleon Bonaparte

Chapter 1

STARTING AT THE BEGINNING

"With the historian it is an article of faith that knowledge of the past is a key to understanding the present."

— *Kenneth Stampp*

As I sat down to write this book, one of the things I struggled with the most (once I actually started, which was a struggle in itself!), was where to start—how to start (jelly on the wall).

"Writing intellectual history is like trying to nail jelly to the wall."

— *William Hesseltine*

It's easy to write about something new when one is the expert. It's going to be easy for me to write about the ideas I want to share with you, about living consciously in the twenty-first century, and of the experiences that have led me to these ideas. However, when it comes to the topic of the history of life, we are all experts, because we each have our own experiences. There are as many versions of history as there are countries, and there are as many versions of how life works as there are people living! You, as you read this, bring to the reading your own unique interpretation of these words.

I hope your heart, mind, and soul will hear my words with the passionate and infinite love that I hold for you and all that exists in this third-dimension, physical realm. I hope you will receive these words with an open mind.

We can bring upon ourselves much agony if we care to study the true accountings of the settling of America, or the slave trade, to name just two of the thousands of atrocities that have taken place on this planet. As a species, we humans have shown ourselves capable of horrendous deeds—against each other and all that crosses our path. I may be overstating it, but it is my impression that most of our hideousness is hidden from us by those in power. History books get edited, the atrocities downplayed or omitted. Recently, I saw a movement by some radical faction claiming the Holocaust didn't happen. Practicing the same tactics practiced at that time: Just keep telling them what you want them to believe and eventually they will believe.

As Napoleon Bonaparte's quote, "History is a set of lies agreed upon," suggests, what we know of history is generally only what the powers that be have decided to tell us.

"If you tell a big enough lie and tell it frequently enough, it will be believed."

— Adolf Hitler

"By the skillful and sustained use of propaganda, one can make a people see even heaven as hell or an extremely wretched life as paradise."

— Adolf Hitler

There might come a day when the knowledge of the Holocaust is lost to the ethers because the powers that be decide to delete those chapters from the history books. But what has already been lost from the history books?

How do we create peace and harmony when there are people who believe what happened did not happen, what is real is not real—who have interpreted the information they've received to arrive at conclusions that can only be described as fringe, illogical, or crazy? What is happening in our world of social media and instant messaging? How easy is it with today's technology to rewrite history or create new fallacies?

We've had some great examples lately. A woman who, as an elected official, decided to rewrite state and federal law by refusing to issue marriage licenses to people she didn't like based on her own personal beliefs. She used her position of power to try to change the law of the land. Social media enabled that woman to garner the planet's attention. Not only did she get her fifteen minutes of fame (and then some), but she received the support of a number of other people—including presidential candidates. Only a tiny fraction of humanity agreed with her, but she had enough supporters to perpetuate a message of hate, to raise money for her in the name of hate. These people are living their lives in fear and they have no idea they are doing so.

Or how about the completely fraudulent attack against Planned Parenthood? People used technology to create false videos showing things that never happened, conversations that never took place. Total lies—yet there will likely always be people now who think the worst of that organization.

For me, there's no clearer indicator that humanity has lost its collective mind than when we see acts of hate.

Time and time again, we hear one version of a story, only to find out days later that nothing that was reported was true. A hero, "murdered while chasing three suspects," is really some crazy lunatic who staged his suicide and was pathological and criminal. A person with a Go Fund Me account to raise money for his cancer treatment is revealed not to have cancer. A child writes a book about a past life he remembers, but it's really a hoax. I could go on and on.

I remember when I was a child in school—the entire study of history made me ill because it didn't match up with what I knew in my heart we are supposed to be doing here on this planet. When we were asked to memorize the years of certain wars, it literally made me sick to my stomach, and I refused to do it. One argument I used to avoid such memorization was that I didn't see any value in cluttering up my head with information I could look up in a history book if I ever needed to know in which year some war took place (which for the life of me I couldn't fathom needing to know—I didn't know about *Jeopardy* at the time). I hated the argument that we learn history so we don't repeat it; how blind the people must be who believe such a statement! Every war repeats man's incessant quest for power and dominion over others, feeding the culture of hate in its self-service, to wage war.

The other problem I had, which I was never comfortable expressing, was that we shouldn't be remembering wars. As a kid, I was still trying to sort out my weird relationship with the world. Because I have always known, with every fiber of my being, that we're here to love, the fact that I was having to learn about wars and other horrible things really troubled me beyond measure. History can be about so many things, but the focus was always on power and conquest.

"We make our world significant by the courage of our questions and the depth of our answers."

— Carl Sagan

If we came here to experience Heaven on Earth, why is it that the very earliest humans didn't get along? Some would suggest that we became erect so we could fight each other better. How sad. How untrue that just has to be.

Given my studies, Darwin's premise of "evolution" is flawed, since our Parental ISness and our creative Oneness created us and everything we see. So while there is an appearance of evolution as it is commonly held, there are enough things that can't be explained that go to support alternate views. One need only study the radial jaw shark (helicoprion) to see that evolution can't be the only answer. Clearly, that was a design that didn't work, and it wasn't the result of any "evolution." "Who thought of that?" is the question that always comes to my mind when I see such unusual creativity! But I may be getting ahead of myself here. Suffice it to say at the moment that there is a lot of disagreement as to how humans came into being, thus my questioning of evolution.

More likely, something like chaos or discontinuity occurred, similar to Noam Chomsky's discontinuity theory about the development of language. There is also a lot of disagreement overall about how language arose or what the first language was. Science tells us the first humans arose in what would be the region now called Ethiopia. That would suggest that all languages (some 6,000 now) stem from one language (with an estimated origin of perhaps 100,000 years ago), but given how science is constantly finding and revealing new theories, that's probably not how things really went down. We may never know.

Starting at the beginning—a slippery slope indeed! It is like nailing jelly to the wall!

We tend to think of original humans as spear-throwing, warring people. This depiction makes no sense to me since there's safety in numbers and building community seems to be easier than fighting. Since, as you will come to understand, I see us as connected, it's hard for me to think we were so disconnected back in the beginning. Creation in the third dimension is a whole lot harder than we realized when we started out is all I can figure. Something unexpected happened.

Back in the 1920s, some Australopithecus remains were discovered in what is now Botswana. Along with a skull, the material found included tools made from the bones of gazelles, antelopes, and wild boar. The archaeologists working there mistakenly interpreted them as a cache of weapons, while later testing would show the points were used simply for digging in termite holes.

What a perfect example of how difficult it is to know what's real or true. This is why, with everything, you need to take it into yourself, into your core, into your heart, and sit with it, *feel* it, and know for yourself whether it is true for you—or what is true for you. The only way you truly start at the beginning is to go within.

You are a creator, and when you are connected to your Great Parent, all is provided to you and available to you—more than you can ever dream of. This is why what shows up is always something greater than you asked for—as long as when you ask, your heart is in the right place.

Would you love to live in a world where each person created his or her own wonderful life from the inside out, and where there is no need to compete or be afraid?

Can you think of five ways your life would improve if you didn't have to worry or be afraid? What if there is nothing to be afraid of?

Sit quietly and go within. Ask your Inner Guidance System, your Spirit, to lead. Breathe into your belly[1] and quiet your mind. What do you feel when asked the question, "What if there is nothing to be afraid of? What would I do if I had nothing to be afraid of?" Listen to your answers and write them down here:

---

1 See "Learning How to Breathe" in the Supplement at the end of this book.

1)

2)

3)

4)

5)

*"Yesterday's the past, tomorrow's the future,
but today is a gift. That's why it's called the present."*

— Bil Keane

ROOTING AROUND IN YOUR CHAKRAS

"The body never lies."

— Martha Graham

The body is made up of different energy systems. One of those systems is the Chakra System. There are many philosophies about the chakras. (We won't be covering philosophy because this is a handbook.) It's important you have a working knowledge of your body, and the chakra system is an important energy system. In Volume II, we'll take a look at our energy systems in closer detail and we'll go into chakras in more detail, but because of the structure of this handbook, you'll also get a little bit about chakras throughout all three volumes.

This handbook is structured with the chakra system in mind: There are seven main sections and seven chakras; each section moves higher energetically, as do the chakras.

What I am presenting to you here is simply one overview of the chakras, and a fairly high level overview at that. It is enough to know what you need to start, or so I hope. This is simply my overview, based on the numerous chakra studies I've had. Try not to get bogged down in the details. If you've had some different teachings, go with what resonates for you.

Throughout the chapters in each section, there will be chakra sub-chapters.

Around each of us is what is called the torus energy pattern (you can Google that and look at images, there are also images on the handbook website). In that energy pattern, there is a flow that comes up our spine and passes out through the tops of our heads and, similarly, flows downward. We get our energy several ways. One is up from Earth/Gaia/Eden through our feet and legs, and another is down from the sky, from the sun, and beyond, through the tops of our heads, from the torus energy pattern that surrounds and envelops Earth/Gaia/Eden and beyond.

As the energy flows up from Earth through our legs, it travels upwards along our spine, raising in frequency as it travels. In the same manner, we will start at the bottom and work our way up in our study of the chakras.

Each chakra is a spinning vortex of energy, spinning clockwise from your left to right. Imagine you are looking at the chakra as a clock on the wall (and you are the wall). When it is balanced, it will spin clockwise—and it will spin counter-clockwise if unbalanced.

There is also energy flowing upward and downward. The flow to the chakras themselves is upward only, according to most authorities. The energy is drawn off to the chakras, and it passes by and spins when it enters the chakra. (Look at the handbook website for images and videos.)

When you are in alignment and your chakras are all open, you are in flow. The energy is coursing through your body, and as it reaches each energy center, it enters, spins around, and exits, moving on, upward, to the next chakra in the flow. If you have a blocked chakra, the flow is interrupted and you are no longer in flow. When this happens, your Spirit and Soul have a difficult time staying in your body because they are connected to the energy of the All That IS, which is in constant flow. When you are blocked, in essence, so are they. Energy is getting trapped and dissipating in its trapped location. Your whole system is being compromised and your flow and connection is being interrupted. You are what some would say is disembodied; disconnected from source.

CONNECTING WITH YOUR ROOT CHAKRA

"There is deep wisdom within our very flesh, if we can only come to our senses and feel it."

— *Elizabeth A. Behnke*

Your root chakra is located at the base of your spine. You should think of it as the base that supports the entire rest of your spine. It is the base upon which your spine sits. Picture the spot between your urethra (or base of your penis) and anus; that is the spot of your root chakra.

This chakra supports your entire body. It rules your basic human instincts for survival, security, and stability. It rules your immune system and kidneys, along with your legs and feet. Emotionally, it governs your sense of loyalty, your survival instincts, and your self-esteem. It's motto is, "I am safe."

Your root chakra's identity is of your physical self, and its primary mission is your self-preservation.

In the days ahead, if you are not already aware of your root energy center, tune into it; pay attention to any sensations you have in this area of your body. Realize that there is an energy flow upward from Earth below you, up through your feet, your legs, to the base of your spine, moving upward, all the way to the top of your head, and outward, upward, into the sky, where it connects with the energy grid that surrounds

Earth/Gaia/Eden. Pay attention to the sensations in your feet and legs and to any difficulty you encounter walking.

You can ask yourself the following questions to access your root chakra:

- How do you feel about your life? Do you feel you have what you need to live comfortably?
- Do you have strong financial foundations, or are you constantly struggling with money and finances?
- Is your current living situation supportive of you? Do you feel valued and respected?
- Do you feel connected to nature?
- Are you easy-going, or do you worry a lot? Are you fearful about the end of the world, or do you know that no matter what happens, you and yours will be okay?
- Do you feel empowered when faced with life's challenges?
- Do you feel you are living life as you want it, or are you more living a life someone else designed for you?
- Do you feel you have enough support where you live?
- Do you have a sense of invincibility? No matter where you are, are you strong and supported?

If you answered positively most of the time, then your root chakra is likely open and flowing. If your answers leaned toward the negative, then your root chakra is quite possibly blocked.

For you, your root chakra is where it all starts. Visualize the base of your spine being strong and an open channel to the energy. See the energy flowing easily up your legs into the base and up your spine. See it happening with grace and the wisdom of the Universe. Know that you are tapped into the One Great Mind, the Mind of All That IS, and you are capable of creating the life of your dreams (assuming you are in alignment with the Good of the Whole).

If you can spend some time with your eyes closed visualizing this flow of energy, take the time to do so as often as you can. See yourself as balanced and strong—vibrant and capable. If you can, stop even for just a few seconds and close your eyes, focus on your breathing, and feel into your root chakra, your base. You will start to connect with this vital region of your body.

"A trembling in the bones may carry a more convincing testimony than the dry documented deductions of the brain."

— Llewelyn Powers

Chapter 2

SORTING OUT THE TRUTH

"You will never find the real truth among people that are insecure or have egos to protect. Truth over time becomes either guarded or twisted as their perspective changes; it changes with the seasons of their shame, love, hope, or pride."

— Shannon L. Alder

What is the truth then, if we can't trust the history books or the news? How do you get to the bottom of what is going on around here? If you can't be sure of the accuracy of news reports, how can you be certain about what you've been told is the origin of life?

"The truth is incontrovertible. Malice may attack it, ignorance may deride it, but in the end, there it is."

— Winston Churchill

There are lots of different approaches to "truth," from philosophy, to psychology, to science, and, of course, religion. This myriad of what is often confusing and conflicting information spans the ages and has led to widely divergent, perhaps even chaotic, life on planet Earth. With over seven billion humans inhabiting Earth, it's hard to see how we can agree on anything given our unique backgrounds and individual perspectives.

Someone tells us there was a big bang; someone else tells us we are a great creation—some people believe in evolution, others in chaos. There are as many opinions as to how things work as there are people. How do you sort out the truth? Who is right? Is it possible that everyone is right? If not, who is wrong?

What if it isn't about who is right and wrong; what if it's about something so much larger, so big, so expansive and amazing, so truly incredible that your head will hurt trying to understand and believe it?

This is what I see, a place where what goes on is magical and miraculous. It's beyond my wildest dreams—the stories I can tell you of synchronicity will blow your mind. I want you to see the world and life as I see it. I want you to know and feel the incredible resources available to you. I want you to know and feel the amazing invisible support system and to know the universe of unlimited possibility that surrounds you.

I want you to understand that every time you step out your door, you are on a magical mystery tour and the Universe wants nothing more than to charm you with synchronicity.

"Lynda, what makes you so certain of these things?" you may be asking. Here's the thing—here's what gives me my depth of faith. I agreed to come to this lifetime to write this book. (Although at the time, I didn't know this is what I would do; I just agreed to come and do some important job that was my assignment.) I was awake for the entire time in the womb, and I remained awake for my birth and for every day since.

It has only been in the past seven to ten years that I could speak easily and openly about my experience. I no longer believe I am unique. There are hundreds of thousands, if not millions, of people waking up and awake.

During that time in the womb, I picked up on a lot of energy here in this realm. Fear, loathing, hate, remorse, disgust, dismay, anger—they all trace back to fear, fundamentally, but what dismayed me was that they existed at all!

This is such an amazing place, but everyone seems so unhappy! Take a moment and check in with yourself—what's the last thing you complained about? How long ago? Honestly now.... Think about the weather, the traffic, the noise, the smells, the crowds, the parking, the road conditions, your family, your classmates, roommate, teacher, boss, parent, etc., etc., etc. Anything come to mind that you've complained about today? Several things? This is what I'm talking about—there is vast, general unhappiness. We are all very clear about what we don't want.

There's a viral video on YouTube of a three-year-old boy crying when he learned about homeless people. That's how I was from the day I got here (although I did not cry out loud). I could feel the sadness on Earth; I was heartbroken over the unhappiness I could feel. I wanted then and still want now for everyone to be happy because happiness and love is what we all came here to experience—it is what explains your existence. No one, not you nor anyone else, came here, in this third dimension to be miserable. We all came here, you, me, everyone else, to be happy—to feel the joy and beauty of love, of sharing, of giving, of helping.

My character is such that I am a caretaker. I am a caretaker of all. My life's agenda is to fix things, to make things right, to tidy up the disarray and to set things straight. It is as if humanity is wandering confused, in the dark. My job here is to illuminate the path to love and peace so that all may find their way.

It took me a long time to stop trying to fix things and people's lives for them. That's a hard lesson to learn—you can't fix anyone. You can't change anyone. You can't "make" anyone do anything or make any one better. (Certainly you can make people do things in work settings, but I am speaking here in more of a "grand scheme of things" context.) You can't make a drunk stop drinking, or a junkie quit shooting up, or an abuser stop abusing. Only those people themselves can make changes in themselves. The only change you can make is to yourself. Only you can change you, and when you do, your world will change.

Back to sorting out the truth—there are thousands of emerging messengers coming forth with books, videos, workshops, and classes—live and on the Internet. Some, because they know religion has alienated people, are attempting to describe what is happening on earth, describe how we as human beings function, and how we can grow, without taking into consideration any concept of "spirit." They are "all up in their heads" as the saying goes. There is a great temptation for those who have been turned off by religion to throw the baby out with the bath water.

What I know to be true is that nothing exists outside of the One Great Mind, our collective Parent. There is something much larger going on here than this third dimensional realm that we exist in. Nothing can be explained correctly without including AAH (God). Without the connection to our Source, Our Shared Parent, nothing can be truly explained.

I have personal knowledge and experience that tells me that we cannot explain what is going on here if we limit ourselves to language and third-dimension thinking. There is a connection to all things; one merely needs to know where to look and how to think to be able to turn one's experience of life from Hell on Earth, to Heaven on Earth.

> *"When I run after what I think I want, my days are a furnace of stress and anxiety; if I sit in my own place of patience, what I need flows to me, without pain. From this I understand that what I want also wants me, is looking for me, and attracting me. There is a great secret here for anyone who can grasp it."*
>
> — *Rumi*

As a child, I would wonder: How many people are out there, just like me, who came into this world with a different perspective from the onset? I remember thinking I was unique, that no one shared my perspective of the fifth and seventh dimensions, or my experience of a really dysfunctional home, or my experience of precognition and psychic experiences.

In time, I came to realize that dysfunctional homes are the norm, and in just the past few years, I have started to find more and more people who have multi-dimensional experiences.

For some people, these multi-dimensional experiences happen all the time, and for some, only occasionally. Interestingly, many people will experience miracles (multi-dimensional experiences), but just chalk them up as coincidences.

How magnificent all our lives would become if we would realize that every miracle is the Universe and Our Shared Parent responding to our needs. As Rumi says, "What you want, wants you, seeks you."

Perhaps this handbook will help bring that realization about in your mind.

A myriad of answers exist to all the questions pertaining to body, mind, and spirit, ranging from psychology and philosophy to religion; and now science is getting in on the act. In actuality, rather than looking to each other for our answers and our truths, we should be looking within ourselves.

"The world is governed more by appearances than by realities, so that it is fully as necessary to seem to know something as it is to know it."

— Daniel Webster

As we go through the coming pages together, take what I illuminate and weigh it within yourself. Listen to and feel how your body responds. Any discomfort you feel is a beacon for where to focus your attention. Your body really is your temple—it knows everything; it is connected to your Great Parent, to the Source of the Universe. It is only you and your ego that get in the way of knowing this.

There is a world of peace, love, and joy awaiting you—awaiting all of us—if we will only try. If my lamp helps you find your way to your inner truth, if my lamp helps you raise your voice and speak your truth, then my efforts will not have been in vain.

If each of us—including you—will find our own internal truth, and live our lives by that, we can get back on track, creating Heaven on Earth.

Can you think of five "truths" you've been taught that you have discovered are false? List them below. How do you feel about these mis-truths?

1)

2)

3)

4)

5)

"All truths are easy to understand once they are discovered; the point is to discover them."

— Galileo Galilei

COLORING YOUR ROOT CHAKRA

"I think we may safely trust a good deal more than we do."

— Henry David Thoreau

The color of the root chakra is red. To bring balance to your root chakra, you can meditate on the color red. Wearing red or surrounding yourself with red is also effective. Eating red foods can also help.

Red is the color of fear and anger. If you have a lot of feelings of fear or anger, your root chakra may be blocked. We'll go into clearing your anger and fears in greater depth in Volume II, but in the meantime, we will spend some time together now laying some groundwork so you have something with which to start.

Close your eyes and visualize the torus energy pattern around yourself. See the energy flowing up from Earth and down from Above. See the color red coursing through, and as you do, recite this clearing statement, "I let go and release everything that causes me fear and anger." Keep repeating this.

Do this for as long as possible, several times day.

A root chakra in good balance is indicated by good health, a sense of trust in the world, and feelings of safety and security, a sense of stability, prosperity.

A root chakra out of balance, or blocked, may be indicated by poor health or a feeling of being disconnected from your body, financial difficulty, poor boundaries, chronic disorganization, or obesity.

You can use the following clearing statements:

- ♥ I release and let go of anything and everything that is stealing my health from me and preventing me from letting go of my feelings of disease.
- ♥ I release and let go of anything and everything that is preventing me from letting go of my feelings of fear and worry.
- ♥ I release and let go of anything and everything that is interfering with my feelings of self-worth and preventing me from being all that I can be.

"Keep attention in the inner energy field of the body as you look around the room. The inner body lies at the threshold between your form identity and your essence identity, your true nature. Never lose touch with it."

— Eckhart Tolle

Chapter 3

DECIDING WHAT'S TRUE FOR YOU

"The first duty of a man is to think for himself."

— Jose Marti

In the last chapter, we attempted to sort out what constitutes the truth. It is a slippery slope, especially when we realize the beliefs that led to the Holocaust were spread by one of the largest scams perpetrated by man against humanity. The Third Reich lied over and over, knowing that if you tell the masses something often enough, regardless of the facts, they will believe you. We are seeing this same attitude being repeated and lived out in today's political arena. The oligarchy is attempting to deceive, misdirect, and co-opt the masses on more subjects than I care to list here.

When did duping each other become commonplace?

"Truth can be stated in a thousand different ways,
yet each one can be true."

— Swami Vivekananda

Perhaps the first thing each of us must decide is where do we want to get our truth from? Whom do we trust?

"The only real failure in life is not to
be true to the best one knows."

— Buddha

When I was growing up in the 1950s, the go-to reference was the encyclopedia—if you were lucky enough to have a set in the house, that was grand; if not, you went to the library where you had a wider variety of reference materials to choose from. The encyclopedia was still a great place to start.

Today, the world is at your fingertips. Just sit down at a keyboard or whip out a phone and Google whatever you want to know about on the big World Wide Web. If we can trust Wikipedia the way we used to trust the encyclopedias, we should be all set. This new way requires a fair amount of vetting, so, as with all information gathered from the Internet, relying on Wikipedia, is probably not as safe as the old encyclopedia.

Here's a perfect example of what we were talking about in the last chapter. You have probably heard at least some of the following statements about our brains:

- Myth #1 — You only use 10 percent of your brain: Now "experts" are saying we use all of our brain.

- Myth #2 — Doing crossword puzzles daily helps keep your brain sharp: Now they're saying it doesn't help.
- Myth #3 — A person's personality displays a right-brain or left-brain dominance: Now they're saying the two sides of the brain are intricately codependent in people and do not influence personality
- Myth #4 — Brain damage is always permanent: Now they're saying the brain can repair or compensate for certain losses and even generate new cells.
- Myth #5 — Drinking alcohol kills brain cells: Now they're saying moderate alcohol use doesn't kill brain cells, and while rampant alcohol use can damage the brain, the damage is not due to cell death.

I can tell you one thing: rampant alcohol use is not good for you. I don't care what anyone says, but I digress.

It's crazy, actually, how many things we've been told were true—were *gospel*—that are now known or claimed to be *not true*.

First, it was butter is bad for you; eat margarine instead. Now it's don't eat margarine, eat butter; it's healthy for you. All these years they've been telling us our cholesterol was linked to our diet; come to find out it's more genetic than anything. Don't eat eggs, only eat egg whites, we were told. Now we're back to: Eat eggs.

Pluto was a planet; now it's a "dwarf-planet," so we don't call it a planet anymore. All those models of the solar system were wrong, all the planetariums, all the maps of the stars.... On and on it goes.

As cited in the last chapter, the "weapons" they found with the Australopithecus bodies in the 1920s were really tools. Mammograms are not as good for you as we thought. We over-treated prostate cancer. Homo sapiens really started in Australia, not Africa.

"When others asked the truth of me,
I was convinced it was not the truth they wanted,
but an illusion they could bear to live with."

— Anais Nin

Over and over throughout history, we have been told one thing is true, only to discover something else is true. Did it start with "The Earth is flat?" No, it started in the Garden of Eden with the snake! What if, from day one, the story of creation has been taught through the egos of humans; what if, from day one, they got that story wrong? But I'm getting ahead of myself; I'll get to that in Chapter 8.

"When I despair, I remember that all through history the way of truth and love have always won. There have been tyrants and murderers, and for a time, they can seem invincible, but in the end, they always fall. Think of it—always."

— Mahatma Gandhi

You are a divine creature, each and every one of you; we are all creations of our great Shared Parent. We are One.

Why are we, as a species, obsessed with looking outward for the answers when, in fact, we are connected to the greatest knowledge that exists—and always have been? We are connected and a part of the Great One Mind that IS. We are the

Great One Mind. We are the All That IS.

Rather than looking around the room for who has a good idea, the only thing that makes any rational sense, once you know this, is to go within! Go within and connect with your built-in guidance system. We are all created connected. If you are not yet aware, you need to know you are connected. You have unlimited power (for the good of the whole) at your fingertips. It is only through a settling of density and a disconnecting from our Shared Parent that we have become so lost and confused as to how things work.

> *"Remembering that you are going to die is the best way I know to avoid the trap of thinking you have something to lose. You are already naked. There is no reason not to follow your heart."*
>
> *— Steve Jobs*

Steve Jobs says it quite well, and in the Walls of Life chapters, we'll delve into all the things that keep us from understanding that the answers to all life lie within us—not externally in the world of the third dimension.

Can you remember a time when you were told something or heard something and it just didn't ring true? Or how about a time when you heard something and all your hairs stood up on end? How about that one?

That rush of goose bumps, which causes the hair to stand up, can happen for a variety of reasons, but the physical reaction is the result of a surge of adrenaline. It is interesting that the mechanism that sends us into fight or flight mode is the same mechanism that gets triggered when we have a soul memory, or other more psychic or intrinsic reactions. Or when we hear "the truth."

Have you had your hair stand on end, or been covered with goose bumps? What is your personal experience with psychic insights or flashes?

1)

2)

3)

4)

5)

"I am not bound to win, but I am bound to be true. I am not bound to succeed, but I am bound to live by the light that I have. I must stand with anybody that stands right, and stand with him while he is right, and part with him when he goes wrong."

— Abraham Lincoln

FEELING YOUR ROOTS
ROOT CHAKRA

"Others show you yourself and what you need to work on within, by their reflection of your own rejected or denied emotions."

— Sandra Weaver

The root chakra rules several areas of your emotional self. Loyalty, survival instincts, and self-esteem are all governed by your root chakra.

Here are some clearing statements:

- "I let go of all issues of loyalty…."
- "I let go of all that makes me feel insecure…."
- "I let go of my fear about what may happen…."
- "I let go of anything and everything that causes me to feel unworthy…."
- "I let go of anything and everything that causes me to feel worthless…." (Unproductive, useless, needy, wanting, lacking, etc.)

And here are some affirmations:

- "I am secure in myself and unafraid of anything."
- "I am secure and safe and feel filled with purpose and worth."
- "I am safe and secure and gladly accept what life has to offer."

"When I dare to be powerful, to use my strength in the service of my vision, then it becomes less and less important whether I am afraid."

— Andre Lorde

Chapter 4

UNDERSTANDING THE MEANING OF LIFE

"Each man must look to himself to teach him the meaning of life. It is not something discovered: it is something molded."

— Antoine de Saint-Exupery

As we saw in the last chapter, as it turns out, truth is really in the eye of the beholder. What is true for you may or may not be true for me. It will depend on whether your experiences result in a shared similarity or reality. Otherwise, we are strangers in a strange land, experiencing different lives through a shared illusion. We are co-creating a shared reality.

What is life then, if we can't be sure what's true? How do we know what we're here for? Where did we come from? What IS the point?

Life, quite simply, is the experience, as the quote above implies. To come here and be in physical form, to share the experience of life as Heaven on Earth with others, to be joyful, loving, and giving, this is the point of life. Life here on Earth/Gaia/Eden is supposed to be Heaven. The pain is not what our Collective Parent ever wanted or envisioned, but once in physical form, humans have tended to do their own thing, through a process we'll be discussing in greater depth in Section 2, Chapter 4. There is what I like to call the Grief of Gravity. It has had what I understand to be an unanticipated effect upon us as a species.

The meaning of your life comes from your response to what happens to you. The lessons your spirit/soul learns from your experiences here in physical form are up to you. This is where free will comes in. Life is always offering you the very best of what is possible. What you don't realize is that everything wants the best for you. You need only be open to receiving the best. Remember that quote of Rumi's? What you want, wants you. What you want is seeking you out!

Your spirit and soul came here to have some very specific experiences. Nothing is random. There is a flow of energy going on. This is one of the essential lessons you must learn if you are going to get the most out of your experience this time around in this physical reality we call *life on Earth*.

There's only *one* thing you have any control over.

The only thing you have control over or control of, is yourself:

- your reaction
- your response
- your reply

- your behavior
- your actions
- your thoughts
- your words

What brings you much agony is your resistance to what the physical world has offered up. What you don't realize is that the pain is necessary for the lesson, whatever the lesson may be. But once the lesson is learned, you never need to experience that pain again, nor will you.

> *"We must assume every event has significance and contains a message that pertains to our questions... this especially applies to what we used to call bad things...the challenge is to find the silver lining in every event, no matter how negative."*
>
> *— James Redfield, The Celestine Prophecy*

In March of 2013, my femur shattered. From the appearance of what happened, I tripped over a piece of ice. I had huge plans for the day. I was mailing the booklets I'd prepared as an overview of WE LOVE US. I was super-excited.

As I lay on the frozen ground waiting for help to arrive, I didn't rail against the world. I lay in happiness, in gratitude that I knew who was coming (my friend is a volunteer EMT and I fell on her shift), in gratitude that there were blankets nearby for my husband to get to put under and around me. A lot went through my mind, but never did a thought of anger or upset arrive.

Life is not about the why; it's about the *what*. It's not about why something happened. Why something happened is *al-*

ways the same. Why anything happens is because it's perfect that it did. I'll explain this concept later in this volume, in detail, but just go with me on this for a moment. Given that it has happened, whatever it may be (from something wonderful to something horrid), *what* are you going to do? How are you going to react? *What* is your response?

You bring life its meaning. The meaning of life is entirely up to you. What do you want your life to be? What meaning do you want it to have? What lessons do you want to leave this life having learned? What legacy do you want to leave behind?

According to Vishen Lakhiani at Mindvalley Academy, our lives have three meanings:

1. What you want to experience
2. What you want to grow in yourself
3. How you want to contribute

What I have always wanted to experience is the peace, joy, and infinite love that comes from Heaven on Earth, which I personally know is what we are here in physical form to experience. I have always wanted this for everyone.

"What I want for myself, I want for everyone."

— Samuel Milton "Golden Rule" Jones

What I have always wanted to grow in myself is the capacity to do just that, bring about the experience of peace, joy, love in my life, and, even more importantly, in the lives of others.

My contribution to life, to humanity, will be this handbook and any subsequent books, workshops, classes, seminars, forums, etc. that help people live their lives to their spirit and soul's highest expressions. To have helped light the way to unity, this is what I want for my legacy.

It is my life purpose to bring all this information into one place, so we can take a look at everything under one lamp, if you will. This is my contribution. I sure hope this book touches you and helps you see how, by making changes within yourself, within your thoughts and actions, you can be living the life of your dreams.

Imagine the world living with these awakened understandings.... Imagine the concepts of love, joy, and peace being taught to our youth, to the children, from the very beginning. The purpose of this handbook is to empower you, the reader, to live a life of Heaven on Earth/Gaia/Eden—to experience an abundance of love, joy, and peace, a life of giving infinite love to all you encounter, to living your life to your spirit and soul's highest possible expression.

What meaning do you want to bring to your life? What do you think is your soul's highest purpose? What do you want to leave behind as a legacy?

Write down five thoughts about what meaning you want your life to have:

1)

2)

3)

4)

5)

"Life is without meaning. You bring the meaning to it. The meaning of life is whatever you ascribe it to be. Being alive is the meaning."

— Joseph Campbell

HEALING YOUR ROOT CHAKRA

"To fear is one thing. To let fear grab you by the tail and swing you around is another."

— Katherine Paterson

Your root chakra is the seat of all your fear. In order to let go of your fear, you must heal or let go of whatever has caused you to become so fearful.

Even the most enlightened and "awake" people are susceptible to feeling fear. Much of this has to do with the fact that we are energetic beings and we emit our energy around us. If you live in a dense area, an apartment building in a city for example, with lots of other people all around you, and all of their energy, then that energy will affect you. Even people vibrating at a high frequency can be affected by people vibrating at lower frequencies. I lived about fifty-five years before I figured out how to manage my energy and become impervious to others' energy.

Clearing Affirmations:

- "I am connected to the energy of Mother Earth. My body, mind, and spirit are grounded, centered, and purified."
- "I am safe. I trust more; I fear less. I am centered and grounded."
- "I am strong, grounded, and protected at all times."
- "I am at peace with the material world in which I live."

You may have some core wounding that will need to be addressed so you can completely clear some root chakra blockages. We'll go into healing your core wounds in greater detail in Section 5. In the meantime, using the affirmations and clearing statements will begin the healing process.

"I've had a problem feeling real all my life."

— Amanda Palmer

Chapter 5

TRACING TIMELINES

"We'll be remembered more for what we destroy than what we create."

— Chuck Palahniuk

Thus far, we've looked at what constitutes truth and what constitutes the meaning of life, but we have not looked at humanity itself, or tried to take a linear look at what most would call the evolution of humanity. How did we, exactly, get from the beginning to where we are now?

Oh, if only there were an easy answer! I just have to laugh at this point. I've been spending a lot of time doing research for this chapter. More time than I care to, actually. And no sooner do I think I'm close to being done than another wrinkle shows up. I feel like I'm playing a game of pin the tail on the donkey—only the donkey isn't a picture on a wall. It's a live donkey, outside in an endless pasture. And yes, I'm blindfolded...stumbling around looking for it.

I was discussing my writings while speaking with a colleague about the beginning of Homo sapiens. His question about the Aborigine population of Australia led me to a more current piece of research than I had found to date that indicates that human beings, our direct ancestors, can be traced to Australia, not Africa, as has been taught for a multitude of years now. After further research, I discovered that it's all up in the air now! Maybe we were everywhere; we're not really sure. As the scientists zero in on DNA studies, more and more information is being discovered, some of it contradictory to what we thought.

So there you go. I better get this book to press. I feel like everything is a moving target!

"History will be kind to me for I intend to write it."

— Winston S. Churchill

As I've said earlier, life is about the experience itself. We came here with a purpose: to create heaven on earth, to love each other, and to experience all that life in physical form has to offer. This I have always known in my spirit and soul. We're a far cry from living the lives we came here to have, and we've been at this for a long time. To make matters worse, even though there are signs all around the world of an awakening of humanity's consciousness, the rampant misunderstandings of real life seem to capture the imagination of the mainstream media, and the awakening is pushed to the back burner.

What is the problem in trying to achieve peace and joy for all? Why is it such an elusive thing?

These have always been my questions: What has happened here? Why is it taking so long to create a paradise of life—heaven on Earth? Did something go wrong? Did we ever have heaven on Earth? Is it possible? If yes, how do we get there from here?

I feel the need to start at the beginning and bring you through time to this moment, so I have created a timeline of what we accept as "history." What I recount below is as accurate and current a version of what has happened since the beginning of time, as we know it, in what may be called the Universe and here on Earth, or Gaia. This timeline has tested my patience. At some point, I simply had to say, "Enough tail chasing!" At that point, I decided to give up listing exact dates and, instead, took more of an overview approach to the timeline.

As previously stated, *history* is what we *agree* it is. We know of numerous things omitted from our school books because the government decided we didn't want to teach our children how horrible we were as a people. Therefore, some of the gory details were left out of U.S. history classes. That's just one illustration of how history is often inaccurate and misrepresented. More incidents of selective history-telling exist than I can possibly recount here. I'll close this thought with the reminder of the tactic Hitler used: "Make the lie big, make it simple, keep saying it, and eventually, they will believe it." We'll leave it at that, for now.

The whole exercise of building this timeline is further proof to me that the truth is an elusive thing, so open to interpretation that it's hard to conceptualize or explain the depth of the difficulty in its determination.

With that being said, I will lay the groundwork. I have done my best to make sure this timeline is accurate, but at this point, I am feeling like both "what's true" and "history" are totally up for grabs. To anyone who wants to take me to task over any inaccuracies, all I can say is I used verified sources. A lot of this stuff is up to either interpretation or change, as scientists perfect their abilities or as things are studied with new technology. Between the time this was written and the time it goes to press, some of these numbers might change. I am not going to try to keep track! By the time you are through it, the point I'm going for will have been made, I think.

The other thing I will say is let's not get too hung up on the details. I'm not trying to prove history, just recap it. When comparing timelines of the same subject, I found repeated differences (of anything from a few years to many depending on when in history).

For example, two websites I used for the religion timelines varied in many, many entries by a few years. I can only presume that the one site was using perhaps the earliest believed date as opposed to a date founded in fact. I started to tear my hair out, but the differences are not important. An approximation is good enough for the purposes of this timeline. I tend to be a perfectionist. At one point, I even considered forgoing the timeline because it was starting to make me crazy and bog me down. But with wisdom comes a kind of surrender. I surrendered to it being good enough to make the point.

Early on in the timeline, many of the numbers are very rough and I have omitted the word *about* to prevent the redundant use of the phrase "about x years ago."

One more note: In later chapters of this handbook, I'll show you how a slightly different mindset makes all the difference in how we interpret events, and how with some rather simple shifts in our way of thinking and perspective, we can radically change our interpretations of events, resulting in an understanding that all is always perfect (even the most challenging things). I will even show you how it's possible to rewrite history at an emotional level, by changing your response in the present. Back to the task at hand—the timeline.

Because Spiral Dynamics is a twenty-first century theory about history, I thought it would be interesting to weave the timeline of history into the periods of history as looked at by the theory of Spiral Dynamics.

One well-known twenty-first-century philosopher is Don E. Beck, who furthered the work of Dr. Clare W. Graves (who worked with Abraham Maslow) with the development of the theory of Spiral Dynamics.

> *"In a nutshell, Spiral Dynamics is a model about human thinking and development—it says that human intelligence is evolving and developing within the context of the world in which we live. Further, that this development is the key to how we perceive and interact with the world—we see the world as we are, not as it is."*
>
> — *Jim Lockard*

Spiral Dynamics presents a worldview of history based loosely on the great story of finding truth: the eight blind men and the elephant. Each blind man, feeling a different part of the elephant, believes he knows the "truth" about the elephant. In Spiral Dynamics, using the idea of eight variations of human and societal development, Mr. Beck has further broken the eight variations into two tiers: Subsistence, which accounts for all of human history up to about 150 years ago, and Being, starting around 150 years ago, bringing us to current times. Portrayed by a colorful upward spiral (Visit the handbook's website WalkingThroughYourWalls.com to find a picture of the Spiral Dynamics model), Mr. Beck suggests that we have moved into the most evolved region of his model, the top of tier two. Original models of the spiral spanned from beige at the bottom to turquoise at the top; more recent models show a ninth color (coral) at the very top of the spiral, as we move into the uncharted territory of a worldview of Oneness. There seems little doubt this is the emerging energy on Planet Earth, Oneness. The world has a long way to go before we are acting from a meme of oneness, but we are certainly moving toward what Mr. Beck calls an "elegantly balanced system of interlocking-forces," and I believe, ultimately, we are moving beyond to true oneness consciousness where we understand the inter-connectedness of all.

According to Spiral Dynamics, the world has passed through the following stages. . .

- ♥ Starting around 100,000 years ago the basic theme or meme was "Do what you have to do to survive," the world consisted of a natural milieu where humans rely on instincts to stay alive ~ **Instinctive/Survivalistic** ~ Natural ~ Hunter/Gatherer ~ The color assigned in the model is beige.
- ♥ Starting around 50,000 years ago, the meme was "Keep the spirits happy and the tribe's nest warm and safe," the world is a magical place alive with spirit beings and mystical signs ~ **Magical/Animalistic** ~ Speech ~ Tool Making ~ The color assigned in the model is purple.

- Starting around 10,000 years ago, the meme was "Be what you are and do what you want, regardless," the world is a jungle where the strongest and most cunning survive ~ **Impulsive/Egocentric** ~ Agriculture/ Settlements. The color assigned in the model is red.
- Starting around 5,000 years ago, the meme was "Life has meaning, direction and purpose with predetermined outcomes," the world is perceived as an ordered existence under the control of the ultimate truth ~ **Purposeful/Authoritative** ~ Law/Order/Religions. The color assigned in the model is blue.
- Starting around 300 years ago, the meme was "Act in your own self interest by playing the game to win," the world is a marketplace full of possibilities and opportunities ~ **Achievist/Strategic** ~ Scientific ~ Instruments/ Machines. The color assigned in the model is orange.
- Starting around 100 years ago, the meme was "Seek peace within the inner self and explore, with others, the caring dimensions of community," the world is a human habitat in which we share life's experiences **Communitarian/Egalitarian** ~ Sensitive ~ Resources/ Civil Rights. The color assigned in the model is green.
- Starting around 50 years ago, the meme was "Live fully and responsibly as you are, and learn to become," the world is a chaotic organism forged by differences and change ~ **Holistic** ~ One World/Information ~ Integrative. The color assigned in the model is yellow.
- Starting around 30 years ago, the meme became "Experience the wholeness of existence through mind and spirit," the world is an elegantly balanced system

> of interlocking-forces ~ **Holistic** ~ Individualistic/Collective. ~ The color assigned in the model is turquoise.

What we appear to be moving into now is the Mystery meme of "We are one with everything and everyone," the world is consciousness, physical reality, an illusion, and we are one with all ~ **Undefined** ~ Oneness. The color assigned in the model is coral.

Visit the website WalkingThroughYourWalls.com to find pictures of the Spiral Dynamics model

Spiral Dynamics gives us a nice framework through which to study history. Each level transcends but includes the previous level. It's easy to feel the energy shift as humans have evolved in body, mind, and spirit.

So, let's take a look at the timeline of the world. I've put this together to illustrate some specific things, so there is no meaning if someone or something you think important has been omitted! If we tried to cover what's important to everyone, we'd be stuck here a long time, and I truly want to move it along after you come to see the salient points of the timeline. Truthfully, even this will take a bit of time.

Here we go:

13.7 billion years ago—From *nothing* there became *something.* From the Void—the ISness—The Great One Mind—from the formless, came forms—The Universe, the beginning of physical matter, best guess, about 13.7 billion years ago. A lot of assumptions must be accepted before one can calculate something like the age of the Universe, and we have no idea how accurate our assumptions are! We know nothing about it, really and truly. But who cares about that? We are humans, so we can just do what we want, say what we want, can't we? That includes writing what we want in the history books. Pick a number, any number. Okay, 13.7 billion years.

8.2 billion years ago—We think the first stars began to shine and the Milky Way was formed. So for some period, the IS-ness was happy with just the Universe and then the ISness thought...hmmm....let's make some stars.... And then some galaxies, solar systems, planets, suns, moons—and eventually, a beautiful, perfect jewel, the best of all the ideas: a planet of an amazing variety of water, land masses, weather systems, atmosphere, gravity.... Perfect—beautiful and perfect.

4.5 billion years ago—Planet Earth formed.

4.1–3.8 billion years ago—Primeval life on Earth began.

600 million years ago—The earliest known fossils we have found are 600 million years old, we think.

300 million years ago—It is theorized that the land mass on Earth formed a super-continent, which began to split apart around 175 million years ago. Which way they split apart is questionable.

4.4 million years ago—The earliest known hominid fossils found in Ethiopia or maybe Australia are this old.

3.2 million years ago—Lucy (Australopithecus Afarenis), the supposed mother of humankind, lived in Ethiopia.

2.5 million years ago—Findings show Homo Habilis (skillful man) exhibits first brain expansion and first tool use.

1.8 and 1.3 million years ago—Homo Erectus was the first of the hominid, or our ancestors, to leave Africa, and this species spread through Africa, Asia, and Europe. (Unless another theory is true and we originated in what is now Australia.)

1 million years ago—Homo erectus developed different skin colors and began to lose its hair.

I will now skip a whole lot of evolution in order to move things along!

400,000 years ago—Aborigines (Homo sapiens) existed in Australia. (It is also theorized that all Homo sapiens came out of Australia, which could make sense if the land split occurred differently than currently taught.)

350,000 years ago—Ancient ruins in what is now northern Israel suggest that fire had become routine.

200,000 years ago—Homo sapiens are found in Africa.

100,000 years ago—In Northern Europe, a mutation arose that disrupted melanin production in the iris and the first blue eyes in a human appeared.

100,000 years ago—It is theorized a single chance mutation occurred in one individual, instantaneously installing the language faculty in perfect or near-perfect form—we don't really know when language began or anything about it.

100,000 years ago—We started making jewelry.

Spiral Dynamics Instinctive/Survivalistic Meme begins: "Do what you have to do to survive," followed 50,000 years later (50,000 years ago), by the Magical/Animistic Meme: "Keep the spirits happy and their tribe's nest warm and safe."

42,000 years ago (40,000 BC)—We were skilled at deep sea fishing in what is now East Timor.

32,100–18,800 years ago—We domesticated dogs from a

group of wolves that came into contact with European hunter-gatherers.

30,000 years ago—We'd spread around the world and were using fibers to make baby carriers, clothing, baskets, bags, and nets.

25,000–8,000 years ago—We painted real art on cave walls.

17,000 years ago—We painted the first boat paintings ever found.

14,300 years ago—The first humans are in North America and in Europe. There is the development of harpoons, needles, and saws.

13,000–12,700 BCE—Pigs were domesticated in the Near East in the Tigris Basin. They were managed in the wild in a way similar to the way they are managed by some modern New Guineans.

10,000–15,000 years ago—We usually think of woolly mammoths as purely ice age creatures. But while most did indeed die out, one tiny population endured on isolated Wrangle Island until 1650 BCE.

11,000–10,000 years ago—The beginning of agriculture, in both the Fertile Crescent and in what would be modern day Iran.

Spiral Dynamics Impulsive/Egocentric Meme begins: "Be what you are and do what you want regardless."

7500–5700 BCE—The settlements of Catalhoyuk develop as a likely spiritual center of Anatolia.

5500–4500 BCE—The Proto-Indo-Europeans (PIE) emerge, probably within the Pontic-Caspian steppe (debated). The

PIE peoples develop a religion focused on sacrificial ideology, which would influence the religions of the descendant Indo-European cultures throughout Europe, Anatolia, and the Indian subcontinent.

3750 BCE—The Proto-Semitic people emerge in the Arabian Peninsula. The Proto-Semitic people will migrate throughout the Near East into Mesopotamia, Egypt, Ethiopia, and the eastern shore of the Mediterranean. Their religion will influence their descendants' cultures and faiths, including the Abrahamic religions.

3700 BCE—Lothal Advanced Civilization in India.

3500–2200 BCE—The armies of Sumer and Akkad are formed (the first recorded armies).

3500 BCE—First written evidence of religion in the world recorded on Sumerian tablets in cuneiform.

Wait a minute. Did you catch that? The same people who developed writing also formed the first armies and religion.... Now that's interesting, isn't it?

3228 BCE—Krishna is born.

Spiral Dynamics Purposeful/Authoritarian Meme begins (given the armies and religions this comes as no surprise, eh?!) "Life has meaning, direction and purpose with predetermined outcomes."

3000 BCE—Egyptians are using papyrus.

3000 BCE—Medicine Wheels are in use in the Americas.

Cultures were simultaneously developing all around the planet.

3114 BCE—August 11 is the start date of the Mayan calendar.

3000–500 BCE—The ancient India culture of South Asia develops.

3000–30 BCE—Egyptian culture develops in northeastern Africa along the River Nile.

3000–350 BCE—Nubian culture develops in northeastern Africa along the River Nile.

2700–1100 BCE—Greek civilizations occur (Cycladic, Minoan, Mycenaean).

2,600 BCE—The step pyramid of Djoser is the first pyramid the Egyptians build.

2400 BCE—The abacus is developed in Babylonia.

2100 BCE to 1CE—Chinese culture develops.

2100 BCE—Ziggurat of Ur, a massive stepped pyramid, is built.

2000 BCE–1200 CE—Mayan culture develops in Mexico and Central America.

2,085 BCE—Judaism is founded by Abraham.

1,500 BCE—Hinduism, with no specific founder, has been practiced for many years prior to this point—prior to Judaism, most agree.

1,400 BCE—or there about—the first written Word of God, the Ten Commandments, is delivered to Moses.

1400–400 BCE—The manuscripts comprising the original Hebrew Bible (thirty-nine Old Testament books) are completed. The Book of the Law is kept in the Tabernacle, and later in the Temple beside the Ark of the Covenant.

1274 BCE—Battle of Kadesh.

1120 BCE—The Sumerian Enuma Elish (creation story) is written.

1100 BCE—Use of iron spreads.

1000 BCE—Three distinct languages emerge: Phoenician was a language originally spoken in the coastal (Mediterranean) region. The Phoenician alphabet was widely adopted for other languages and is ancestral to both the Arabic and modern Hebrew alphabets. The second language was Aramaic, originally spoken in the Fertile Crescent and Eastern Arabia. The third language, Hebrew, is historically regarded as the language of the Israelites and their ancestors. Hebrew ceased to be an everyday, spoken language somewhere between 200 and 400 CE. (A revival in the 1900s CE has resulted in Hebrew being spoken by a total of 9 million people worldwide today.)

1000 BCE—Zoroastrianism founded by Zarathushtra (Zoroaster) in Persia.

1046 BCE—Shang-Zhou War in China.

1020–930 BCE—The beginning of the Kingdom of Israel (united monarchy) occurred sometime between these dates.

900 BCE–200 BCE—Pre-Columbian Chavin people, who dwelled in the highlands of what is now Peru. Monuments include both an "old temple" and "new temple" made of rectangular stone blocks and shaped like flat-topped pyramids.

890 BCE—Approximate date for the composition of the *Iliad* and the *Odyssey*.

800 BCE—The Greek cultures develop (Ancient Greece—Peloponnese, Epirus, Central Greece, Western Greece, Macedon, later Alexandria.

730 BCE—The Persian culture develops in Greater Persia.

753 BCE—Rome is founded.

700–400 BCE—Panini's precise systematization of the Sanskrit language forms the basis of current computer language.

624–546 BCE—Greek philosopher Thales of Miletus discovers static electricity and is often cited as the first philosopher. He believed everything was made from water.

620–550 BCE—Pherecydes of Syros lived, who authored a cosmogony known as *Pentemychos.* He is the most important forerunner of the Presocratic thought.

610–546 BCE—Anaximander of Miletus, founder of the Milesian school. Famous for the concept of Apeiron, or "the boundless."

600 BCE–400 CE—Roman culture develops in Italy. Known for its agriculture, calendar, and concrete. Its language is Latin and its religion is polytheistic.

600–400 BCE—Probable time of Laozi, author of the *Tao Te Ching*, considered the founding work of philosophical Taoism.

600 BCE—Babylonian king Nebuchadnezzar II restores the Ziggurat of Ur pyramid topped with a shrine to a moon god, making it the most well-preserved of the pyramids in the region.

600 BCE—The second development of writing. Several Mesoamerican scripts (writing) are known, the oldest being from the Olmec or Zapotec of Mexico. (This is a separate and independent evolution of writing much later than the original Mesopotamian writing around 3200 BCE.)

At this point, humans are all over the planet; I am going to move things along in terms of this timeline.

600–0 BCE—Philosophers begin to show up in abundance: There were hundreds philosophers in just a 600 year period, ranging in focus from Eleatics to Pluralist to Sophist to Ethics, Politics, Autonimist, Stoicism, and on and on. With written language and paper, everyone has an idea about how life works and can document his ideas, the most famous of this period being Socrates of Athens (c. 470–399) who emphasized virtue ethics. In epistemology, he understood dialogue to be central to the pursuit of truth. Another well-known philosopher from this period was Pythagoras of Samos, of the Ionian School, he believed the deepest reality to be composed of numbers and that souls are immortal. Heraclitus of Ephesus, of the Ionians, emphasized the order and mutability of the universe. Heraclitus of Ephesus, of the Ionians, emphasized the order and mutability of the universe. Democritus, another prominent ancient Greek philosopher, formulated the atomic theory that states that all matter is composed of particles called atoms. Plato is famed for his view of transcendental forms. He advocated policy governed by philosophers. Aristotle was a polymath whose works ranged across all philosophical fields. Aristotle is known as one of the greatest intellectual figures of Western history; he was a Greek philosopher and scientist. He was the author of a philosophical and scientific system that became the framework and vehicle for both Christian Scholasticism and medieval Islamic philosophy. Last, but not least, you have likely heard of Cicero, a political theorist.

Meanwhile…elsewhere in the worlds of religion and war… both have lots of activity.

600-0 BCE—Wars include: the Greek Punic Wars, the Peloponnesian War, the Corinthian War, the Samnite Wars between Rome and Samnium, the Wars of Alexander the Great, the Syrian Wars, and the Punic Wars between Rome and Carthage. Construction begins on the Great Wall of China, and there are the Macedonian Wars, the Cretan War, Roman-Syrian War, Roman Servile Wars, Mithridatic Wars, Julius Caesar's Gallic Wars, Julius Caesar's Roman invasion of Britain, Parthian War of Marcus Licinius Crassus, Caesar's Civil War, the Roman Civil War, and the Chinese War.

600-0 BCE—Religious activity includes Jainism being founded by Mahavira; Siddhartha Gautama (Buddha), founder of Buddhism, is born as a prince of the Shakya tribe; Buddhism is founded by Gautama Buddha; Confucius, founder of Confucianism, is born; and Taoism is founded by Lao Tzu. There's the completion of all the original Hebrew manuscripts that make up the thirty-nine books of the Old Testament, all of the original Old Testament Hebrew books have been written, collected, and recognized as official, canonical books. In the region of central Sudan, once known as Nubia, hundreds of burial tombs are built, mostly out of reddish sandstone. The temple-pyramid complex, Great Pyramid of Cholula, is built in four stages and dedicated to the deity Quetzalcoatl in the region now called Mexico. The third Buddhist council is convened. The Septuagint Greek Manuscripts, which contain the thirty-nine Old Testament books *and* fourteen Apocrypha books, are completed; the oldest surviving Hebrew Bible manuscripts date to about the second century BCE (fragmentary). Perhaps the most significant occurrence of the end of this era was the birth of Yeshua Ben Joseph, the man who would become known as Jesus and Christ, and who would begin the new era by founding a new religion.

First Century CE—Jesus founds the New Covenant in Christ, which eventually becomes Christianity.

c. 33 CE—Crucifixion of Christ.

0-1500 CE—Philosophers abound, only now their focus includes things such as: self-determination, holistic metaphysics, Neoplatonism, pantheism, Islamic philosophy, Jewish philosophy, Ascetic, and Christian philosophy. We will come to see that the crucifixion of Christ becomes a topic of unending interpretation, continuing to modern times and today.

Some names you might recognize from this time period include Marcus Aurelius who was a Stoic, St, Francis of Assisi who was an ascetic, Roger Bacon who was an Empiricist and mathematician, and Thomas Aquinas who was a Christian philosopher. Lesser known are the founders of Modalism (Monarchianism, possibly the original Oneness movement), Sabellius, Praxeus, Noetus, Paul of Samosata, and Marsilio, the first translator of Plato's complete extant works into Latin.

0—1500 CE—Religious milestones include: The original twenty-seven books of the Greek New Testament are written; Gnosticism is formed; the oldest known version of the *Tao Te Ching* is written on bamboo tablets; the Edict of Milan decrees religious tolerance in the Roman Empire; and Jerome's Latin Vulgate manuscripts are produced, which contain all eighty books of the Bible (thirty-nine Old Testament, fourteen Apocrypha, and twenty-seven New Testament). Saint Jerome translates the Hebrew Bible into Latin. By 500 CE, the Bible has been translated into over 500 languages, not limited to, but including an Egyptian version (Codex Alexandrinus), a Coptic version, an Ethiopic translation, a Gothic version (Codex Argentus), and an Armenian version. Some consider the Armenian to be the most beautiful and accurate of all ancient translations. Roman Catholicism becomes the dominant form of Christianity in 590 CE, and from 570–632 CE, Muhammad ibn 'Abdullāh lives. The Roman Catholic Church declares Latin as the only language for scripture. In 610 CE, Muhammad receives his first revelation on Mount Hira and founds Islam. The verses of the Qur'an are compiled in the form of a book in the era of Uthman, the third Caliph of Islam. In 1205, Stephen Langton, theology professor and later Archbishop of Canterbury, creates the first chapter divisions in the books of the Bible. In the fifteenth century, the Rosicrucians are allegedly founded by Christian Rosenkreuz.

0-1500 CE —Wars and conflicts of this era include: The Roman conquest of Britain, Queen Boudica's Uprising, the Yellow Turban Rebellion, the Vandal War, and the Saxon Wars. Then there is the Norman conquest of England, the First, Second, Third, and Fourth Crusades (spanning 1096-1204), the Mongol wars and conquests, the Fifth Crusade, the First Barons' War (England), the Sixth, Seventh, Eighth, and Ninth Crusades (ending finally in 1272), the First War of Scottish Independence, the Peasant revolt in Flanders, the Polish-Teutonic War, the Hundred Years War, Hussite Wars, and the Wars in Lombardy. This period ends with the Thirteen Years War that started in 1454 and the Wars of the Roses that began in 1455 and didn't end till 1485.

0-1500 CE—Meanwhile, elsewhere in the world of discoveries, inventions, and the arts: the first mechanical clock is built, the first movable type printing press is built, the Magna Carta is signed, Marco Polo begins his travels to Asia, and Thomas Aquinas writes *Summa Theologica*. The first eyeglasses are made, the Renaissance begins in Italy in the 1300s, and Inca culture develops in Ecuador, Peru, and Chile. Aztec culture develops in present day Mexico, the Bubonic plague (Black Death) spreads in Europe, and the first suspension bridges are built. Chaucer writes *The Canterbury Tales,* the Incan Empire is formed in Peru, and Gutenberg invents the alphabetic printing press. Books may now be mass-produced instead of individually handwritten. The first book printed using the new press, is Gutenberg's Bible in Latin. Ending this era, in 1492, Columbus reaches the New World.

1500–1600 CE—More and more philosophers emerge, including but not limited to theories of free will, realism, utopia, skepticism, heliocentrism, Cartesian, Pyrrhonist, Empiricist, dualism, rationalism, and numbers theologians. Some notable names include Desiderius Erasmus, Niccolò Machiavelli, Sir Thomas Moore, Martin Luther, John Calvin, René Descartes, Baruch Spinoza, and Isaac Newton.

1500-1600 CE—Religious developments include: Protestantism founded by reformers Martin Luther, Ulrich Zwingli, and John Calvin; Martin Luther initiates the Reformation in 1517 and translates and publishes the New Testament for the first time into German from the 1516 Erasmus version. William Tyndale produces the first translation of the New Testament from Greek into English in 1525. Dropping its 1,000-year-old, Latin-only policy, the Church of Rome produces the first English Catholic Bible, the Rheims New Testament, from the Latin Vulgate. In 1582, Pope Gregory XIII reforms the calendar.

1500-1600 CE—Wars include: the Ottoman Civil War, the Spanish conquest of the Aztec Empire, the Inca Civil War, the Spanish conquest of the Inca Empire, the Conquistador Civil War in Peru, the Russo-Swedish War, the Burmese-Siamese War, the Eighty Years War, the Ottoman-Venetian War, and the Russo-Crimean War.

1500-1600 CE—Elsewhere in developments around the world: Michelangelo begins painting the Sistine Chapel, the first pocket watch is made, Machiavelli writes *The Prince,* Magellan's expedition circumnavigates the globe, Ether is invented, and in 1543, Copernicus postulates a heliocentric universe. The ironclad warship is first developed, the pendulum is invented by Galileo, and he also invents the thermo-scope.

1600-1700 CE—In this 100-year period, the world of religion included these events: The King James Bible is printed, originally with all eighty books, Tibetan Buddhism is established by the Dalai Lama, Rosicrucians are founded, in what is now referred to as North America, by Master Kelpius and Johann Andrea.

1600-1700 CE—In this 100-year period, there were at least fifteen major wars, including the Polish-Swedish War, the Dutch-Portuguese War, the Thirty Years War, the Pequot War, the Franco-Spanish War, and the Beaver Wars (Iroquois). The First English Civil War, Second English Civil War, Third English Civil War, First Anglo-Dutch War, Anglo-Spanish War, Peach Tree War (Susquehannock), King Philip's War, Great Turkish War, Nine Years War, including King William's War, and the Jacobean Rising in Scotland.

1600-1700 CE—Elsewhere in world developments: Shakespeare's *Hamlet* is produced. Cervantes writes *Don Quixote,* the first modern novel. Jamestown Colony is founded. The first telescope is invented, and Galileo is the first to point it skyward, making the first astronomical observations. The first real thermometer (as opposed to thermoscope) is developed, as is the first slide rule. The Pilgrims land at Plymouth Rock. Descartes publishes *Discours de la Méthode.* The first adding machine and first barometer are invented. The

Taj Mahal is completed. The first vacuum pump, first sealed liquid-in-glass thermometer, and first pendulum clock are invented. Newton publishes his theory of universal gravitation and Milton his *Paradise Lost*. Issac Newton discovers calculus. The first pressure cooker is created. Leibniz's calculus and Locke's *Essay Concerning Human Understanding* are published. The first steam engine is built.

Spiral Dynamics Achievist/Strategic Meme begins: "Act in your own self-interest by playing the game to win."

1700-1800 CE—More Philosophers emerge, with theories of Malebranchianism, politics, determinism, utilitarian, materialism, idealism, humanism, genetic determinism, atheism, feminism, and anarchy. Well-known names include: George Berkeley, Voltaire, Immanuel Kant, Moses Mendelssohn, Edmund Burke, and Thomas Jefferson.

1700-1800 CE—Religious developments included: Freemasonry is founded by Albert Mackey and Albert Pike, Swedenborgism founded by Emmanuel Swedenborg, Shakers founded by Mother Ann Lee, and William Young prints the first pocket sized "school edition" King James Version Bible in America.

1700-1800 CE—More wars, at least sixteen major ones, including the Great Northern War, the Tuscarora War, the First Fox War, the Yamasee War, the Chickasaw Wars, the Second Fox War, the War of Jenkins' Ear, King George's War, and the French and Indian War (part of the Seven Years War). Also, the Seven Years War, the Anglo-Cherokee War, Pontiac's War, the American Revolutionary War, the Chickamauga Wars, the Anglo-Spanish War, the Northwest Indian War. The French Revolution and the Haitian Revolution, and in 1776, the U.S. issues its Declaration of Independence. In 1787, the U.S. Constitution is signed; freedom of religion is enshrined in the Bill of Rights, amended into the Constitution of the United States, forming an early and influential secular government.

1700-1800 CE—Inventions and discoveries include: the first piano, the first steam piston engine, and first mercury thermometer. Bach completes the Brandenburg Concerto. The Celsius Scale is developed. Benjamin Franklin discovers the first lightning rod. Johnson publishes the *Dictionary of the English Language*. In 1760, the Industrial Revolution begins in England. Mozart (aged eight) writes first his symphony. Watt patents the first practical steam engine. Adam Smith writes *The Wealth of Nations.* Rounding out this hundred years are the first hot air balloon, first steamboat, and first vaccination.

1800-1850 CE—Philosophers and philosophies include evolutionary theorists, determinists, conservatism, socialism, idealism, pessimism, transcendentalism, abolitionism, egalitarianism, humanism, transcendentalism, pacifism, existentialism, and anarchy. Well-known philosophers during this time include: G.W.F. Hegel, Arthur Schopenhauer, Ralph Waldo Emerson, Charles Darwin, Søren Kierkegaard, and Henry David Thoreau.

1800-1850 CE—Religious developments include: birth of Bahá'u'lláh, who later founds the Bahá'í Faith, Mormonism is founded by Joseph Smith, Campbellites is founded by Alexander and Thomas Campbell and Barton Stone; and Tenrikyo is founded by Miki Maegawa Nakayama. Phineas P. Quimby begins his work in New Thought; Millerites Second-Day Adventists are founded by William Miller; Christadelphians is founded by John Thomas; Seventh Day Adventists founded by E.G. White, and Spiritualism is founded by Kate and Margaret Fox.

1800-1850 CE—Wars in this fifty-year period, more than twenty-two, include: the Napoleonic Wars, the Russo-Persian War, the Rum Rebellion, the Spanish American wars of independence, the Mexican War of Independence, the War of 1812, the Creek War, the Seminole Wars, and the Zulu Wars of Conquest. The Texas-Indian wars, the Greek War of Independence, the Comanche-Mexico War, the Java War, the Winnebago War, the Black Hawk War, the Texas Revolution, the First Opium War, the Navajo Wars, the Mexican-American War, and the Apache Wars.

1800-1850 CE—Discoveries, inventions, and the arts include: the first locomotive, the first stethoscope, the discovery that electricity can make magnetism, and the discovery that electricity and magnetism used together can make a force. The first electric motor is built, the first mechanical computer designed, and photography is invented. The idea of resistance in the realm of electricity is developed, the first lawnmower is built along with the first combine harvester and first refrigerator. Braille is invented, the first revolver made, and Morse code is invented. The electric telegraph is developed, rubber is vulcanized, and electricity is proven to be a kind of energy. Anesthesia is first used, the first typewriter and first sewing machine are made, the Absolute Temperature Scale or Kelvin Scale is discovered, and the first safety pin is made.

Spiral Dynamics Communitarian/Egalitarian Meme begins: "Seek peace with the inner self and explore, with others, the caring dimensions of community."

1850-1900 CE—Philosophers are now abundant, far too many to count, in the areas of egalitarianism, abolitionism, anarchy, utilitarianism, idealism, pragmatism, existentialism, feminism, and Darwinism among others. Familiar names include: Sojourner Truth, Karl Marx, Friedrich Engels, Susan B. Anthony, William James, Friedrich Nietzsche, Sigmund Freud, and G.E. Moore.

1850-1900 CE—Religious developments include: The Apocrypha is officially removed from The Bible in 1885, leaving only sixty six books; Jehovah's Witnesses is founded by Charles Taze Russell; the Theosophical Society is founded by H.P. Blavatsky and Henry Olcott; Christian Science is founded by Mary Baker Eddy, and the Unity School of Christianity is founded by Myrtle Fillmore.

1850-1900 CE—Wars during this brief period include: the California Indian Wars, the Crimean War, the American Civil War, the Snake War, Red Cloud's War, the Comanche Campaign, the Great Sioux War (Black Hills War), the Nez Perce War, the Cheyenne War, the Sheepeater Indian War, Victorio's War, the Boxer Rebellion, the Second Boer War, and Europe colonizes the African continent.

1850-1900 CE—Inventions, discoveries, and the arts include: First mechanical submarine, revolving machine gun, dynamite, the stock ticker, and the gasoline carburetor. Alexander Graham Bell patents the telephone. The microphone is invented, along with the phonograph, and the Cathode Ray tube. Edison developed his electric light. The photophone is developed, the motorcycle is invented, and the world's first skyscraper is built in Chicago. Alternating current systems gained further viability with introduction of a functional AC motor, the first zipper is designed, wireless communication is developed, and New Zealand becomes the first country to grant women the right to vote. The first diesel engine is built, radio signals are discovered, the first remote control made.

NOTE: Breaking the philosophers up into three periods over the next 100 years became too difficult because of overlaps of lifetimes, so several memes have been lumped together in the 1900—2000 "philosophers" section below. The next Spiral Dynamics meme starts around 1950, and the next meme around 1970.

1900-2000 CE—Philosophers abound, hundreds, perhaps even thousands, covering the realms of pragmatism, existentialism, logical positivism, pacifism, Marxism, phenomenalism, Hermeneutics, Akashik Records, and Integral Theory, to name a handful. Some well-known names include: George Santayana, Bertrand Russell, A.O. Lovejoy, Pierre Teilhard de Chardin, Jean-Paul Sartre, Ayn Rand, Simone de Beauvoir, Wilfrid Sellars, Albert Camus, Noam Chomsky, Don Beck, Ervin László, and Ken Wilbur. There are more people with ideas and philosophies about how life works than can be counted at this point.

1900-1950 CE—War and other developments include: the Russian Revolution, the Mexican Revolution, World War I, the Russian Civil War, the Turkish War of Independence, the Irish War of Independence, the Chinese Civil War, the Spanish Civil War, World War II (millions of Jews are relocated and killed by the Nazi government during the Holocaust), the Greek Civil War, and the Arab-Israeli War. Atomic bombs are dropped on Hiroshima and Nagasaki, the first meeting of the U.N. General Assembly takes place, Churchill's "Iron Curtain" speech marks the beginning of the Cold War, Gandhi's civil disobedience movement leads to an independent India, and the Arab League launches modern pan-Arabism.

1900-1950 CE—Religion continues to grow with the following developments: the Rosicrucian Fellowship is founded by Max Heindel; the ancient language Hebrew is revived, which results in it being spoken by a total of 9 million people worldwide today; in France, the law on the separation of church and state is passed, officially establishing state secularism and putting an end to the funding of religious groups by the state. The Pentecostal Assemblies of the World are formed; Rudolf Steiner founds Anthroposophy as a new religion; Iglesia ni Cristo, an international Christian religion that originated in the Philippines, is founded by Felix Manalo; and the International New Thought Alliance is founded. Oneness Pentecostalism is founded by Frank Ewart, G.T. Haywood, and Glenn Cook; the True Jesus Church is founded by Paul Wei, Lingsheng Chang, and Barnabas Chang; Ernest Holmes founds Religious Science; Alice Bailey founds the Arcane School; *The Science of Mind*, the chief textbook of Religious Science, is published; Mind Science founded by Ernest Holmes; the Assembly of Yahweh is the first religious organization in the Sacred Name Movement; Black Muslims (Nation of Islam) is founded by Wallace D. Fard; Guy W. Ballard (1878-1939) starts the "I AM" religious movement; The Way International funded by Victor P. Wierwille is founded; Latter Rain is founded by Franklin Hall and George Warnock; and Jews return to their ancient, biblical homeland and the state of Israel is created. The World Wide Church of God is founded by Herbert W. Armstrong, the Self Realization Fellowship is founded by Paramahansa Yogananda, and Silva Mind Control is founded by Jose Silva.

1900-1950 CE—Elsewhere around the world: the first vacuum cleaner is built, the first powered airplane made, Einstein announces his theory of relativity, and the helicopter, radio amplifier, and color photography are invented. Picasso's Les Demoiselles d'Avignon introduces cubism. Bakelite is invented. Rutherford discovers the structure of the atom and announces it is mostly space. Ford develops the first moving assembly line. Sanger founds the international birth control movement. The global "Spanish flu" epidemic happens. The first sound film is made, the electro-mechanical television system is developed, and Farnsworth demonstrates the working model of a television. Lemaitre proposes the big bang theory. The first antibiotics are developed, and penicillin is discovered. Hubble proposes his theory of expanding the universe. The U.S. stock market crash precipitates global depression. The first jet engine is built. The first ballpoint pen is created. The Aqualung is developed, and so is the encryption machine and a decoding machine. The first electronic computer, ENIAC, is built. The first microwave oven is built. Train and automobile travel become commonplace. Modern/Western medicine becomes an establishment.

Spiral Dynamics Holistic Integrative/One World meme begins
"Live fully and responsibly as what you are and learn to become."

1950-1969 CE—Wars continue including: the Korean War, Mau Mau Uprising, Cuban Revolution, Algerian War, Vietnam War, and the Bay of Pigs Invasion.

1950-1969 CE—Religious developments during this era include: Scientology is founded by L. Ron Hubbard; Wicca is publicized by Gerald Gardner; the Unification Church is founded by Rev. Sun Myung Moon; the Institute of Divine Metaphysical Research is founded by Henry Kinley; the Church Universal and Triumphant is founded by Mark and E.C. Prophet; and Henry Kinley begins the Institute of Divine Metaphysical Research (IDMR). Various Neo-Pagan and New Age movements gain momentum; Transcendental Meditation is founded by Maharishi Mahesh Yogi; Unitarian Universalism is formed from the merger of Unitarianism and Universalism and The Church of All Worlds; the first American neo-pagan church is formed by a group including Oberon Zell-Ravenheart, Morning Glory Zell-Ravenheart, and Richard Lance Christie. The Vatican sends a letter which becomes known as the "Crimen sollicitationis" to all pertinent parties that there are specific guidelines for dealing with any church person engaging in sexual abuse of parishioners; Eckankar The Ancient Science of Soul Travel (Eck) founded by Paul Twitchell; the Assembly of Yahweh is founded by Jacob Meyer; the Church of Satan is founded by Anton LaVey; the International Society of Hare Krishna is formed; and Children of God is founded by David (Moses) Berg. This just scratches the surface. Many self-proclaimed prophets emerge.

1950-1969 CE—Around the world: Abstract expressionism is introduced, the nuclear power reactor is developed, DNA's structure is discovered, Brown v. Board of Education begins the unraveling of U.S. racial segregation, the first optical fiber and first video cassette recorder are made. The Russians launch Sputnik and Sputnik 11. The U.S. lands on the moon. The first silicone chip is manufactured. Mary and Louis Leakey uncover hominid fossils. Other first include the laser, optical disk, computer mouse, ATM machines, hypertext, and video game console. In 1969, Armstrong and Aldrin walk on the moon, and ARPANET (the Internet) is developed by the U.S. Department of Defense.

Spiral Dynamics Holistic Individualistic/Collective meme **begins** "Experience the wholeness of existence through mind and spirit."

1970-1999 CE—Wars during this period include: the Soviet war in Afghanistan, the Iranian Revolution, which results in the establishment of the Islamic Republic of Iran, the Iran-

Iraq War, the Falklands War, the Gulf War, the Croatian War, and the Kosovo War. The El Salvador War, Lebanon Conflict, the Invasion of Grenada, the Tanker War, the Invasion of Panama, the Somali Civil War, Intervention in Haiti, and the Bosnian War.

1970-1999 CE—Religious developments include: the Findhorn Community is founded by Peter and Eileen Caddy and David Spangler; Jane Roberts publishes the first volume of her channeled Seth Material; Divine Light Mission is founded by Guru Shri Hans Ji Maharaj; The Maharishi initiates a "world plan" to introduce Transcendental Meditation to the entire world; CARP (The Collegiate Association for the Research of Principles) is established in the United States to introduce the teachings of Sun Myung Moon, and the Assemblies of Yahweh founded by Sam Suratt. Numerous religious leaders are accused of impropriety, including embezzling and lavish personal display, including but not limited to Jim and Tammy Bakker and Jimmy Swaggart. *A Course in Miracles*, which contains "channeled information" received by Helen Schucman, is published; J.Z. Knight begins channeling Ramtha; the Church of Christ International is founded by Kip McKean; Shirley MacLaine publishes *Out on a Limb* and the *Out on a Limb* television miniseries is broadcast; Deepak Chopra meets the Maharishi and joins Transcendental Meditation; the Tara Center is founded by Benjamin Crème; the House of Yahweh (Abilene) is founded by Jacob Hawkins; and *The Aquarian Conspiracy* by Marilyn Ferguson, sometimes called the "New Age Bible," is published. Ramtha's School of Enlightenment is founded; the Silver Scrolls, believed to be the oldest Bible text ever, is found; James Redfield publishes *The Celestine Prophecy;* and Deepak Chopra publishes *Ageless Body, Timeless Mind: The Quantum Alternative to Growing Old;* after

Chopra's appearance on *The Oprah Winfrey Show*, he sells 130,000 copies of the book in one day. (Winfrey also boosted the career of Marianne Williamson, an advocate of the program *A Course in Miracles.*) Chopra teaches Ayurveda, a form of Indian folk medicine, and his book *The Seven Spiritual Laws of Success* claims that humans can be healed from all problems by opening themselves to the flow of the single source of universal energy.

(I find it incredibly interesting that in spite of the brilliant information that Deepak Chopra and others brought forth during this time period, it continues to languish in implementation. Here it is, many years later, and instead of each of us embracing the single source of universal energy and becoming the creators that we truly are, we choose as a whole to remain in a competitive mindset manipulated to a large extent by capitalism.)

1970-1999 CE—Meanwhile, in the world at large, these things were happening: Internet protocol (HTTP) and HTML code are invented along with a plethora of other technology starting with things like 8-track tape and reel to reel to cassettes. VHS wins out over BETA, CDs and DVDs replace tape, and MP3 and MP4 files replace those. Video games, digital answering machines, text messaging, beepers and pagers, cell phones, GPS, and drones are invented and move us into a dizzying speed of growth and change. Email is invented, along with liquid crystal displays, pocket calculators, and floppy disks. Ethernet networking is invented. Smallpox is eradicated, and scientists identify AIDS. The camcorder is invented. The fall of communism happens in Eastern Europe. Presidents and other political figures engage in sessions with psychics like Jean Houston. The Internet and world wide web begin to change the way we communicate, the way we do business, and the way we live. It is a digital revolution, and by the end of the century, the advance in technology has begun to blur the lines of privacy and government oversight.

Spiral Dynamic 9th Mystery meme of Wholeness Consciousness begins: "We are one with everything and everyone."

2000 CE to Present—Since we have yet to find our way to peace, the wars and military actions of the twenty-first century thus far include: U.S. War in Afghanistan (which according to Wikipedia, continues at publication, as does U.S. involvement in Iraq, and Operation Inherent Resolve), the Iraq War, the War in Somalia, military intervention in Libya and the Gaza War. Numerous clashes in the Middle East continue; it's hard to keep track of the conflicts. Terrorism grips the planet; the fear of it is especially high in the United States after the terror attack of 9/11/2001. Numerous terrorist attacks occur around the world. The United States also faces a "war on guns" as domestic deaths from assault rifles in the hands of the criminal and/or mentally unstable becomes a growing problem.

2000 CE to Present—Religions and Oneness movements really take off; multiple and varied movements of interfaith and oneness, mindfulness and meditation gain momentum. New religions are abundant, and circles begin to crop up with more frequency as a way of coming together, offering an alternative to traditional religious gatherings. Increased reports of sexual abuse of children by clergy and staff and accusations of a cover-up completely rock the Catholic Church. In April 2010, in response to extensive negative publicity and criticism of the pope, the Vatican enters what the Associated Press calls "full damage control mode." Humanity's Team is created by Neale Donald Walsch, spiritual author of the *Conversations with God* series of books, and on the solstice, December 21, 2012, Conscious Evolution welcomes the Birth of a New Era, founded by Barbara Marx Hubbard. The Catholic Church faces the resignation of a Pope and the newly selected Pope Francis laicizes and excommunicates a pedophile priest.

2000 CE to Present—Around the world: Big pharma comes into its own, dominating television commercials with ads to fix everything from sexual problems to restless legs to demanding bladders; "there's a pill for that" becomes a standard joke. Many cancers are cured, and an addiction to pain killers and heroine takes over the United States. The technical digital age takes over the world, and the way we communicate, the way we do business, watch movies, watch television, the way we play games, the way we exercise, the way our homes and vehicles work, along with the way we listen to music, changes. In fact, because of the way computers and operating systems work, we have entered an era of continual change, growth, and expansion. Digital satellite radio is invented, the discovery of Eris, an astral body 27 percent larger than Pluto, trumps Pluto, to become the ninth largest body known to orbit our sun. Its discovery prompts a redefinition of the term "planet," and Pluto is reclassified as a dwarf planet. The discovery of Eris is the trigger that changes the face of our solar system, defining the planets and adding Pluto to a growing family of dwarf planets. Mary Higby Schweitzer and colleagues discover what appear to be soft tissues inside a fossilized T-rex femur. Scientists confirm the existence of "dark matter," even though they still can't explain what it is. Exoplanets are finally confirmed (after detection in the 1990s); these alien worlds have been seen orbiting distant stars by two observatories. Cyborgs are becoming reality, with numerous robotic limbs being controlled by their owners or wearers' minds. Stem cell research takes a huge leap when two different sets of scientists discover they can use adult skin cells, and by essentially turning back the clock, the cells became pluripotent cells, or cells that can end up being virtually any other kind of cell. Water is discovered on the planet Mars, leading to further speculation of microbial life there. The human genome is mapped along with dozens of other species, including pigs, dogs, bees, mosquitoes, puffer fish, chimpanzees, yeast, corn, and rice. Climate modelers admit they were wrong in their models and now project that Europe's glaciers are likely to be entering their final decades; the snows of Kilimanjaro and other low-latitude mountains could disappear completely, and there will likely be ice-free summers in the Arctic Ocean. Rising ocean levels cause low-lying coastal areas to reevaluate their futures. Climate changes around the globe make the news on a regular basis. On and on it goes.....

Some of the most recent and significant developments include:

On July 4, 2012, the discovery of a new particle with a mass between 125 and 127 GeV was announced; physicists suspect it is the Higgs boson (a particle predicted to exist since the 1960s but never seen until now).

On December 1, 2015, an article cites recently published studies of Professor Ajit Varki at the University of California-San Diego School of Medicine, who found intriguing evidence of uniquely human gene variants. "We unexpectedly discovered that humans have evolved gene variants that can help protect the elderly from dementia."

On December 15, 2015, two teams of physicists, working independently at CERN, reported preliminary hints of a possible new sub-atomic particle; if real, one possibility is that the particle could be a heavier version of a Higgs boson. (In my theory, this discovery brings us one step closer to scientists understanding that consciousness is everywhere and in everything. Consciousness is all there is.)

Okay, we are caught up in time to the end of the year before publication of this book—enough of this timeline. What strikes you the most?

Are you exhausted? I know I am. It was exhausting researching this timeline because conflicting information, which seemed to be a rather constant occurrence, kept me chasing my tail. Every once in awhile, though, there would be a new jewel, like the article I found that was just hours old about us being New Humans (next to last entry in timeline). And every once in awhile, there would be a complete heartbreak. (An author I highly regard and his journals may or may not be legit.)

You see, life is a moving target, isn't it? No matter how sure you might be about something, you can likely find someone who will disagree with you, or some new information to dispute what you know. This is one of the points I will remind you of numerous times: If you want to know the truth, you need to go inward. Everything you need to know is accessible from within yourself. In Section 2, we will go into this concept in more detail, and in Volume II, we will go into it in depth.

What strikes me the most about the timeline is that life tends to come down to three things:

- Advancement of life (science, inventions, the arts)
- Theories about life (religion/philosophy)

- The protection of life and the acquisition of territory (war), which was also often based on beliefs (religion).

As there were more people, there were more ideas of how life works, which led to more conflicts and disagreements, more things to fight about.

I hope it became clear that just about everyone has some idea of how to explain what's going on in life, some theory, philosophy, or religion. Humans have been seeking answers since the beginning of time. And lots of people think they "know." There were numerous light bringers before Yeshua Ben Joseph came along, and there are more modern day light bringers than can be counted.

In essence, it seems like what all of life revolves around is whose idea(s) you decide to believe and killing those who disagree with you. Forgive my bluntness. There are thousands of religions and philosophies; there are hundreds or thousands of self-declared "messiahs" or people who believe they have all the answers and should be followed. The further we go along, the more people there are, the more theories, the more choices, the more reasons to disagree and fight—the more reasons to feel isolated and alone.

If only we were all aware of the Akashic Records, or The Book of Life. Theorized throughout the ages, the Akashic Records is the One Great Mind; it is the knowledge of all that is; it is your soul's history and memory, and mine; it is the history and the future of the Universe and all that is. Akasha, which is Sanskrit for "primary substance," is the energy that makes up everything in the Universe. Every vibration that occurs in the Universe through our thoughts, words, and deeds creates an indelible imprint on the Akasha, leaving an energetic recording of every creation, of every soul, of everything. This is why

I am repeatedly suggesting you have everything you need to know within you; you have direct access to the truth.

By the time I was nearing the end of the timeline, I became aware of a feeling of despair that had overcome me. Life seems to have become a dizzying array of conflict over theories. I could see and feel what the many people who have no hope see and feel.

I have a dear friend, a woman, who as a college student worked as a housekeeper one summer for the lodging business my husband and I manage. She's a young mother and is considering enlisting in the military. In our discussion, she made this statement: "There will never be peace."

Those words cut me to my core. But after going through this timeline, I can at least understand how someone can think there can never be peace. (Let me say, right now, that it's extremely important we never make such statements, especially with emotion or intent, which we'll get into in Section 2, the Supplement, and Volume II.)

It's easy to see how depressing life can seem, though. It's easy to see how one might think that things will never change, that things can't ever change. It's easy to see how life can seem without hope.

But one of the last entries on the timeline was hopeful. The article talked about how, as a species, we know how important our elders' knowledge is, so our bodies adapted so we could keep their minds strong longer. That's pretty amazing. Consider what the possibilities are.

Actually, what I think happened is that we, as a species, knew that we needed the elders coming up—the elders of what are currently the Awake movement (the ones who have managed to navigate life successfully, without this handbook)—to retain their memories; therefore, we had to adapt to whatever third-dimension physical influence has been interfering with our memories.

Our ability to adapt is one thing; how and why we adapt is another. While Darwin may have identified some aspects that might apply, there is something much more powerful than traditional evolution occurring in humans. Put another way, in my language, our Great Parent knows that dementia creates more problems than it cures, so the Great Parent has adapted us to eliminate dementia, except for those whose souls choose the experience for a learning tool.

Let's move on for now.

Here's my very favorite timeline nugget. I didn't embed it above because I really wanted to savor it.

David Hawkins was a new age author and philosopher who developed a Scale of Consciousness around 1990 CE. He coined the term Homo Spiritus as an evolved human with Jesus Consciousness. Technically, I believe that would make one a Homo sapiens Spiritus.

Hawkins' theory involved using kinesiology (muscle testing) as a way to determine your state of consciousness. He also linked frequencies or hertz, to the frequency or vibration of our bodies.

Here's a brief overview of the Hawkins Scale of Consciousness:

Although Hawkins' original scale went from zero to 1,000, later work has expanded the scale to Infinity. Someone who body tests at Infinity using kinesiology would be someone with God Consciousness. Someone testing at 500,000 would be an Archangel.

Hawkins Original Scale:

Level	Log
Enlightenment	700-1000
Peace	600-700
Joy	540-600
Love	500-540 (528 hertz is the "Love" frequency)
Reason	400-500
Acceptance	350-400
Willingness	310-350
Neutrality	250-310
Courage	200-250
Pride	175-200 (200 = 40 hertz[2])
Anger	150-175
Desire	125-150
Fear	100-125
Grief	75-100
Apathy	50-75
Guilt	30-50
Shame	below 30

2 The scale also maps to sound frequency; Hawkins' work suggests staying above 40 hertz.

I personally know there are now many people testing at Infinity on the Hawkins Scale of Consciousness, and likely scores of folks in the 700-1000 range, with another huge number at the "love or above" level (528 hertz on the sound scale).

"Together we must learn how to compose difference, not with arms, but with intellect and decent purpose."

— Dwight D. Eisenhower

Doesn't this bode well for what lies ahead—that so many people are testing at Infinity, and so many others are testing at "love or above?" It is incredibly exciting, and certainly nothing I would have predicted when I sat in metaphysical circles back in the 1980s and 1990s. It's so beautiful to me that the movement I thought was fringe back then has actually gained the momentum to help create an awakening in humanity and assist with the reconnection of the self to Source.

What excites me the most is the opportunity we have for me to shine my unique light with you so that you too might look at the timeline and see it the way I do (when I look through my eyes, not the eyes of a researcher)—as an interesting documentation of the game of life we are playing here in this third dimension. To look at it and laugh at the craziness instead of crying over the insanity. To look at it and smile at the lunacy instead of weeping over the waste. To look at it and see how it is perfect, in that it has led us to this moment in time: you and me conversing here in the handbook about life and how we are learning to live it consciously; how we are waking up after so many years of living asleep.

What were the most interesting things to you in the timeline? Why are they interesting?

1)

2)

3)

4)

5)

"History cannot give us a program for the future, but it can give us a fuller understanding of ourselves, and of our common humanity, so that we can better face the future."

— Robert Penn Warren

SINGING TO YOUR ROOT

"When your energy vibrates at a frequency that is within direct alignment to what the Universe has been attempting to deliver your entire life, you begin to live in the flow and true miracles start to happen."

— *Panache Desai*

The tone of the root chakra is "C" or a hertz of 261.6 (between neutrality and willingness on the Hawkins Scale). You can sing songs that use the tone of C, and you can also listen to tonal music. There are a number of different frequencies, chakra tones, and songs using Solfeggio frequencies available.

I am a big fan of making up songs. I sing in the car, and any time I find myself alone, you might find me singing an affirmation or clearing statement. I don't sing random things; everything I sing is picked for the power of the tones or words.

Try singing some of these clearing statements for your root chakra; just make up a tune you like or sing these phrases to a tune you already know and like:

- ♥ I release and let go of anything and everything that is causing me fear and anxiety.
- ♥ I am happy and safe, standing firmly on my two legs.
- ♥ I release and let go of any and all things that cause me to feel unstable.

"My heart is like a singing bird."

— *Christina Rossetti*

Chapter 6

DECONSTRUCTING RELIGION

"The Christ-symbol is of the greatest importance for psychology in so far as it is perhaps the most highly developed and differentiated symbol of the self, apart from the figure of the Buddha."

— Carl Jung

I hope you found the last chapter on timelines interesting and revealing of a view of life not quite seen before. I found it especially interesting that the timeline can be basically summarized by science/discovery, religion/philosophy, and war. Compiling that timeline was further proof of how elusive and changing the "truth" is.

"The devil can cite Scripture for his purpose."

— William Shakespeare

Although I tried to trace the evolution of religion in the timeline, I think, because of religion's power and the huge role it plays in our lives, it bears some further attention.

One finds, in this task of "deconstructing religion," that you can end up chasing your tail because one definition is based on a previous usage, which may be based on a different definition, sometimes in a different language, and on and on you go. Just like the "truth" in other studies, the truth is especially elusive in religious studies.

"I like your Christ. But I do not like your Christians. They are so unlike your Christ."

— Gandhi

Words and names we commonly use today did not exist in ancient times, and, of course, no one was around to write down what happened during the early years that are documented in the Bible, so how exactly did it get documented? Where did the original stories of the Old Testament and other ancient writings come from if the people who wrote them down weren't there to witness them?

The Bible and many other religious texts are bandied about as if they are the gospel truth, when, in fact, they are the creations of men, not our divine Parent. Nothing humans express is pure; everything is filtered through the vessel that delivers it. Our personal experiences influence our delivery.

We don't know much about religion prior to written records, and it seems all the studying of ancient religion revolves around burial traditions. We have to start somewhere, I suppose....

"There is no need for temples, no need for complicated philosophies. My brain and my heart are my temples; my philosophy is kindness."

— Dalai Lama

It is not my intention to go through all the different religions for you, or in any way to judge any of them as right or wrong or of one being more worthy than another. They *all* exist at a level beside, outside, or apart from what I want to show you. I am shining the light on all of it, with the hope of revealing things in a new illumination.

"Anyone who thinks sitting in church can make you a Christian must also think that sitting in a garage can make you a car."

— Garrison Keillor

I want to take you to the place where you have opened up to the broadness and diversity that our humanity brings to this physical third dimension. I want to take you to the place of the beginning, to the truth that resides inside all the teachings, to the hidden jewel that will show you the way to your joy, which is the only thing that truly matters because when you are in your joy, you are one with the Unified Field and All that IS. When you are in your joy, you are one with all that is and you are connected to the Oneness of our Heavenly Parent.

You see, it isn't just the issue of any one of these things: religion, time, space, philosophy, science, etc. It's *all* of them because all of these things are connected, and you are connected to all of it, and to me, and to everyone and everything else.

There are as many theories and ideas about these things as there are people who study them. When you look at any religion, it has a theory of how life works, how life came into being, and what life means. Everyone has a theory! In fact, a new Christian denomination is being established every ten-and-a-half hours!

"All outward forms of religion are almost useless, and are the causes of endless strife. Believe there is a great power silently working all things for good, behave yourself and never mind the rest."

— Beatrix Potter

What I have found is that when studying science, the most current one is the most relevant. On the other hand, when studying spirituality and religious philosophy, while there may be nuggets of truth in some modern work, it all tends to be clouded with the influences of this physical plane and, in too many cases, the authors' egos.

In the end, most religions, philosophers, and systems miss the ultimate gift that our Shared Parent gave us, which is the ability to feel, create, and share joy and to experience bliss, peace, and love. We are certainly free to feel other things (pain, misery, loathing, greed, hate, etc.), but why would we choose these things, as we do so often? No one comes here with the intention of living a life of misery; unfortunately, many live lives of misery and pain because they do not understand how things work. But I'm getting ahead of myself.... Back to deconstructing religion.

As with the different dimensions of being, we find many dimensions within religion—and every one of them has a theory about how things work.

One of the research paths I was following was the term "Ascended Master," which led me to a Wikipedia article[3] with the following statement:

> A "Lord of the World" is a human being (or a being of some lifewave other than the human lifewave) who has taken the Ninth Initiation. The Ninth Initiation is the highest Initiation possible on a 9d-dimensional planet grid such as Earth and it will be until the end of the 21st of December 2012.

That's lovely, except it doesn't say what happens *after* December 21, 2012! And how do you know what they're talking about with the Ninth Initiation in a 9d-dimensional planet grid? As if they teach this stuff anywhere! Gee whiz! You can find out what a 9d-dimensional planet grid is by Googling it, but for the Wikipedia definition to include the phrase—as if we all know what it means.... Well, you see where I'm going.

We've all lived through the "end of the world" Mayan Calendar, 12/21/12 now. Does that make us all Ascended Masters now? To the visual eye, nothing happened!

That's to the visual eye. To my eyes, and to the eyes of many involved in the Awakening of Planet Eden, much is seen. There is definitely a shift in consciousness occurring—definitely an awakening happening.

There is an awakening that is manifesting across all sorts of fronts, from political, to environmental, to spiritual, to financial, to economic, to agricultural, to pharmaceutical, to medical, to scientific. I could go on. It's been happening for quite some time now, in a visible way, but if you take a wider angle

3 https://en.wikipedia.org/wiki/Ascended_master

view, you will see, as I do, that a great and perfect evolution is occurring here on Earth/Gaia/Eden with us humans.

Back in October of 2010, I attended Jon Stewart's Rally to Restore Sanity.

I'm glad I attended because I witnessed one of the largest turnouts Washington, D.C. has ever experienced. The rally generated the highest ridership of the D.C. Metro on a Saturday in the history of the line. (I got that from insider's information, but it likely will never be publicly admitted.) There were people on the mall, all the way to the Washington Monument, and I witnessed the largest media conspiracy ever perpetrated upon the American people, in person, firsthand.

The media were told not to attend by their employers; reporters and the like were informed that if they did attend the rally, they were not to report on the event. There was no major channel media coverage except what occurred on social media and some cable channels; the mass of humanity did not hear our voices, did not know hundreds of thousands of people, perhaps even a million or more, were willing to travel thousands of miles to attend and show their support for a more tempered and moderate approach to our problems as a country.

When the mid-term elections took place that November, apathy prevailed, voter turnout was low, and gerrymandering on the part of the Republicans (Rethuglicans as some would call them) took care of the rest.

I am convinced that had the mainstream news channels covered the Rally to Restore Sanity, the mid-term elections in 2010 would not have gone as they did. The fringe conservatives would not have won the seats they won. But sadly, a deep and profound apathy has set in throughout this country, and too many people believe their voices don't count so they can't make a difference. You could not be more mistaken. It's supposed to be "government of the people, for the people, by the people," so if we're not happy with the government, we have no one to blame but ourselves. Later on, in Volume III, we will go into more depth on this subject, but in the meantime, let me just say that if you are of voting age and eligible to vote, no matter where you live on this planet—go and register, and make sure you vote in every election you possibly can. You must make your voice known. Be heard.

For me, December 21, 2012 didn't change anything instantly; rather, it marked the doorway, standing open, through which I gladly passed, along with many others. It is what marks a transitional time for me as I embraced the mission I came here to do. As I understand it, thousands, perhaps hundreds of thousands or even millions, walked through their own doors at this same time. So, while 12/21/12 was not a visible "end of the world," as some predicted, it most certainly marked a new world being born.

So let's get on with this, shall we? There's so much ground to cover!

There is One Mind, One Supreme Source from which All That IS came. It is often called the Mind of God, and we are often asked to call this "The Father" or "Our Father." As you have seen, I am using Universal Parent, Heavenly Parent, Celestial Parent, and Our Great Shared Parent as substitutes for the gender-laden term "father."

The IS-ness which is us started out without gender. It started out in a non-material way. It started out as thought before form; it did not have a sex. One may presume the application of gender came about much later, in a male-dominated society, when they came to talk about this IS-ness.

When the man Yeshua Ben Joseph made reference to his "Father," he was referring to his Creative Parent, or what we think of today as "God."

According to globalresearch.ca, the word "God" never appears in the original language of the Bible. According to the dictionaries, God is from the sixteenth century German. Instead, such words as Yahweh, YHWH, Elohim, Ho Theos, or Ho Kurios were used in the original Scriptures. The word's only surviving non-Germanic relative is Sanskrit "hu."

Numerous sources seem to back up this claim. In fact, the English word "God" is identical to the Anglo-Saxon word "good." There is a great article to read if you want to understand more about the word God itself, by Craig Bluebell on the site Bible Answer Stand.[4] He leaves us with the question "What do we now do with the knowledge that our word for God is rooted in pagan, astrological worship?"

Regardless of the origin of the word god, throughout history, cultures have had deities they worshiped. Egyptians, for example, had a multitude of gods and goddesses from Aker to Yam (or Yamm), including the god Aah! (I chose the word AAH for God, never knowing about this Egyptian god!)[5] Across the globe and throughout time, cultures have had deities they called "gods" for everything imaginable—gods ruling the skies, the earth, and all things in between.

---

4 http://www.bibleanswerstand.org/God.htm and http://www.bibleanswerstand.org/God_2.htm

5 http://www.landofpyramids.org/aah.htm, http://www.landofpyramids.org/names-of-egyptian-gods.htm, http://www.newworldencyclopedia.org/entry/Yam_(god)

The seat of civilization has been traced to South Africa (or is it Australia? We're not sure). But original aboriginal cultures tend to be the happiest people on Earth/Gaia/Eden today. As I've said, it's truly impossible to know the beginnings at this point, from any external source. Nothing was written down for thousands of years after numerous religions had already started.

It's also entirely possible that long before Christ, the damage of disconnection from our Source had already occurred. By the time Yeshua Ben Joseph arrived here on Eden/Earth/Gaia, it might have already been too late for his message of love to be heard. Human beings were so steeped in fear already—already so capitalistic, corrupt, materialistic, and conniving. Certainly, Yeshua's reception (execution at such a young age) is a good indication that he was too late.

Yeshua Ben Joseph came here in that lifetime to try to help turn things around, to try to reconnect humanity with the Celestial Parent, to show the way to harmony and love, to show the way to reconnect with Source—to show the way to peace and oneness. He came to wake us up.

I believe at this time on earth there are hundreds of thousands, if not millions, awakened individuals walking this planet, giving voice to these same callings. Giving voice to infinite, unconditional love, giving voice to peace, giving voice to joy, giving voice to self-care, giving voice to compassion, giving voice to oneness, giving voice to mindfulness, giving voice to transcendence. However, there are some distinct differences in approach that I want to point out. I am serving as a luminary. I am merely shining a light on the road in the darkness. I am not suggesting anyone follow me; I am not attempting to lead you down a road. I have swept up into a pile the answers to many of the questions about life you may have. My unique life and ability to find answers has resulted in my being able to shine a light on things in such a way as to make them easier to see. That's all. I'm *not* attempting to start a new religion as Yeshua Ben Joseph inadvertently did or as many others have throughout the ages.

I believe you have all the answers you need within yourself, and you don't need to follow anyone but your own spirit and soul. We will talk about this in greater detail later on in this volume and in Volume II.

Let's spend just a little time looking at the current religions on Planet Earth and at the influence they have on modern society.

As a starting point, here is data that was current as of December 2015. How lucky for us—when I found this article it had been updated just four hours earlier! Thank you to the Religious Tolerance Group for this up-to-date post.[6]

6 http://www.religioustolerance.org/worldrel.htm

Basic information on various religions:

Religion	Date Founded	Sacred Texts	Membership	% of World
Christianity	30 CE	The Bible	2,039 million	32% (dropping)
Islam	622 CE	Qur'an & Hadith	1,570 million	22% (growing)
Hinduism	1500 BCE—with truly ancient roots	Bhagavad-Gita, Upanishads, and Rig Veda	950 million	13% (stable)
No religion	No date		775 million	12% (dropping)
Chinese folk religion	270 BCE	None	390 million	6%
Buddhism	523 BCE	The Tripitaka (consisting of the Vinaya, the Sutras, and the Abhidharma)	350–1,600 million	6% (stable?)
Tribal Religions, Shamanism, Animism	Prehistory	Oral tradition	232 million	4%
Atheists	No date	None	150 million	2%
New religions		Various	103 million	2%
Sikhism	1500 CE	Guru Granth Sahib	23.8 million	<1%
Judaism		Torah, Tanach, and Talmud	14.5 million	<1%

Spiritism	None cited		12.6 million	<1%
Taoism	550 BCE	Tao-te-Ching	12 to 173 million	<1%
Baha'i Faith	1863 CE	Alkitab Alaqdas	7.4 million	<1%
Confucianism	520 BCE	Lun Yu	6.3 million	<1%
Jainism	570 BCE	Siddhanta, Pakrit	4.3 million	<1%
Zoroastrianism	600–6000 BCE	Avesta	2.7 million	<1%
Shinto	500 CE	Kojiki, Nohon Shoki	2.7 million	<1%
Other	Various	Various	1.1 million	<1%
Wicca	800 BCE, 1940 CE	None	0.5 million?	<1%

Additional notes on Taoism—According to a statistical overview in 2011 of religions in China: "The number of Taoists is difficult to estimate, due to a variety of factors including defining Taoism. According to a survey of religion in China in the year 2010, the number of people practicing some form of Chinese folk religion is near to 950 million (70% of the Chinese). Among these, 173 million (13%) practice some form of Taoist-defined folk faith. Further in detail, 12 million people have passed some formal initiation into Taoism or adhere exclusively to it."[7]

Religioustolerance.org notes that: "Taoism and Confucianism (mixed with Buddhism) are major cultural and philosophical influences in many East Asian nations. Religious Taoism in still very significant in Taiwan."[8]

7 http://www.religioustolerance.org/worldrel.htm
8 http://www.religioustolerance.org/taoism1.htm

ChartsBin.com reports 6,111,056 Taoists as of 2006.[9]

Patheos.com and ReligionFacts.com report 20 million followers of Taoism.[10] [11]

Estimates are, at this point in time, that there are at least 4,200 or more religions on Earth with, as you can see, the top three being: Christianity, Islam, Hinduism.

Here is a very brief summary of six of the best known religions: Christianity, Hinduism, Buddhism, Islam, New Age, and Judaism—just so we have some basis for discussion.

> **Christians** believe in a God who is loving and approachable.
>
> > There are currently 43,000 denominations and this number is expected to grow to 55,000 by 2025, according to Gordon-Conwell Theology Seminary.
> >
> > It is estimated that a new denomination is formed every 10.5 hours, or 2.3 denominations per day. (Mind boggling, isn't it?)
>
> **Hindus** acknowledge multitudes of gods and goddesses.
>
> > Hinduism has been called the oldest religion in the world, and many practitioners refer to Hinduism as "the eternal law" (Sanātana Dharma).
> >
> > There are six generic types of Hinduism and thirty or more subsets or denominations.

---

9 http://chartsbin.com/view/pog
10 http://www.patheos.com/Library/Taoism
11 http://www.religionfacts.com/taoism

Buddhists say there is no deity.

> Five basic types of Buddhism.
>
> Many subsets—too many to count.
>
> Some would say there are as many types of Buddhism as there are Buddhists.

Muslims (Islam) believe in a powerful but unknowable God.

> Three major sects. The subsets are hard to count—perhaps as many as thirty-five or more.

New Age followers believe they are God because God is in All There Is.

> There are easily 350 or more New Age denominations. (Of personal note, only one in the list had the word love in the title! This is important, as you will learn further on.)

Judaism today is not so much a religion as a cultural heritage, although it began as a very significant religion because of its focus on monotheism.

> Jews are members of the tribe of Judah, also known as Israelites, members, and direct descendants, of a nation existing in the land of Israel from the sixth century B.C. to the first century A.D., and one whose religion was Judaism.

Religions are fluctuating in power. Some radical factions of Islam are still using war as a way to spread their religion. Peace is elusive in the Middle East, no matter how hard people work at it. But peace is elusive everywhere.

As a side note regarding the elusiveness of peace: We have two primates that are our closest cousins—chimpanzees and bonobos. No bonobo has ever killed another bonobo. We don't know why that is. But what we think of as sex is something completely different in their world. Bonobos use sex as a negotiation and comfort technique, and they all have sex with each other regardless of age and gender. They live peacefully, and there is no murder. Whereas, there is murder among chimpanzees, our other cousins, and they tend to lead warring lives. The question is: Is it our genetics or our beliefs that cause us so much pain and suffering?

"Before you speak to me about your religion, first show it to me in how you treat other people; before you tell me how much you love your God, show me in how much you love all His children; before you preach to me of your passion for your faith, teach me about it through your compassion for your neighbors. In the end, I'm not as interested in what you have to tell or sell as in how you choose to live and give."

— Cory Booker

One has to wonder, what exactly is religion giving us? We have roughly a *different religion* for every 1.6 million people. Religion is not solving our problems. Every year, we're gaining about 76 million people (that's total births minus total deaths); we're creating, on average, 2.3 new religions a day!

Religion is not bringing us or giving us peace. Religion is not showing us how to solve our problems. All religion is doing at this point, from what I can see, is serving as one more way to divide us and give us something to argue over. It's not getting us to love. It's not leading us to peace. It's not bringing us joy.

Given the number of Christian denominations and the speed with which they are multiplying, combined with all the other religious factions, rather than achieving Oneness, or peace, or love, we seem to be generating a dizzying array of ideas that seem to fuel the fear and loathing climate—the hate and hysteria, the division and derision.

It has always seemed to me that the *only* way to solve the problems on Earth/Gaia/Eden, the only way to find some unity, the only way to find our way to Oneness, would be to go back to the beginning and figure out what happened. How did we get here?

When I traced things back, I discovered the concept of god has existed since the beginning of time because it means something so much more than most people understand.

The sound "god" means the creator or supreme being (Our Great Parent); it means the All That IS because AAH is the sound of space. We all think that it's quiet out there, but it's not if you have the right "ears." NASA has developed instruments to measure the electromagnetic vibrations of space,, and these instruments have recorded the sound AAH in our solar system.[12]

This is why I suggest the use of the term AAH to replace the word god. Because the word god is not meant to be a word—it is meant to be *a sound*!

I will never forget the feeling I had when this bit of information became clear to me. I had been doing what I do—studying, studying, studying, finding that thread and teasing it out. Then the rest of the time I was meditating on what I

12 http://canyouactually.com/nasa-actually-recorded-sound-in-space-and-its-absolutely-chilling/

was studying and learning. When the idea crystallized, I got goose bumps from head to toe. It's about the sound!

Language evolved from sound to written words. The sound of things came first; then we figured out how to capture the sound in written form. So the word god is meant to replicate the *sound* of the One Great Mind. It is my belief that the word god, or Jah & Yahweh in Hebrew, Allah in Arabic, perhaps even Krishna in Hindi, and Jehovah in the Old Testament are meant to replicate the sound of the Universe. They all contain the sound of AAH within them.

The sound of the Universe, the sound of the One Great Mind and Parent, is the sound of *love*.

Aaahhhhh. The frequency of 528 Hz (the heart frequency). This is what I believe the "origin" of the word god to be—the sound that it replicates.

Before we had language, we had sounds. All these names have the aaaah sound in them: YAHweh, AllAH, KrishnAH, JehovAH, JAH, GAHd. That can't be a coincidence; there are no coincidences.

If you are interested, you can find numerous versions of 528Hz on YouTube.com. If you look for "Solfeggio 528," you will find a variety of productions. There is a whole range of frequencies. The higher frequencies move upwards through the chakras to the crown and above to the Universe.

For many years, I have been adamant that if we want to learn to communicate with each other peacefully, we must stop using the word god—stop using all religious words—because religious words are the words of dogma…dogma gone awry for many at this point.

We may be using the same *word*, but we *all* have different meanings for the word *god*.

I don't intend to offend the religious people reading this! But can you honestly say there is no problem with the language of religion today? How can we ever find common ground upon which to stand and work together if we continue to use the same language that has gotten us to this point of separation and fear? As Albert Einstein said, "We cannot solve our problems with the same thinking we used when we created them."

> *"You never change things by fighting the existing reality. To change something, build a new model that makes the old model obsolete."*
>
> *— R. Buckminster Fuller*

Perhaps this handbook is the new model. I'm not asking or suggesting that anyone give up his or her religion. All I am asking is that you open your mind to a broader understanding and scope. Open up to the possibility that there may be multiple ways to get to heaven—that your way, if you have one, might not be the only path. Open up to the possibility that the way to find peace is to embrace an interfaith approach, to embrace something outside all religion, that we can *all* agree upon. Open up to the possibility that because the teachings we've been handed down through the ages were written by human beings in this third dimension, there may be some inaccuracies, mistakes, or even disasters.

Isn't it possible, just as I have demonstrated with all the other research, that there may be some errors in the ideas we've been led to believe? Isn't there a chance that some folks along the way didn't quite understand life and how it truly works, and by not understanding life themselves, have misled the rest of us? Perhaps not on purpose, but by accident? Isn't there a possibility someone with personal or financial motives has modified the truth? History has shown it is possible, over and over, in war and politics. Isn't it possible the same thing has happened in our religious teachings? Don't we owe it to ourselves to ask these questions?

I hope you will be open enough to recognizing that many people have rejected religion because of the judgments they feel. I ask you to be open enough to acknowledge we have a problem facing our planet in the form of a division among people, and that no one religion seems capable at the moment of bringing about the sweeping changes of love and peace that we need. It doesn't even seem feasible that any existing religion has enough members to overpower the others. (Thank goodness!)

Isn't the incredible speed with which we are creating new religions a clear sign we are lost?

Even if you feel comfortable and confident in your religion, can you see from the table of religions, that there's no way anyone is going to win this discussion?

So what do we do? Many people give up right here!

It is difficult for us as humans to stop and actually think when we are faced with something as huge as overcoming the problems of the world and finding a way to make peace with each other; most of us just give up thinking. It's too huge. It makes your head hurt, so you stop.

I happen to be gifted with the ability to know that the pain in my brain is my brain actually working. So instead of pulling back from the pain, I push into it. It's like walking into the wind. You put your head down and your shoulder into it. Wallace D. Wattles, in his book, *The Science of Getting Rich*, says that sustained thinking is the hardest thing we are asked to do as humans. Or as Henry Ford said, "Thinking is the hardest work there is, which is the probable reason why so few people engage in it."

But serious, sustained thought is how all great inventions have been made. It is the power of creation. Most people stop thinking the minute their heads start to hurt. Instead, you should think of the pain the way you would if you were working out. You don't get off the StairMaster or treadmill the minute it starts hurting. You push into it, but with your brain, you stop, don't you? Think of what you might do, learn, or be if you learn to push into it?

So my question to you is: Can the idea of interfaith live? Are we capable of putting some of the religious details aside to allow us to find a more common ground upon which we can all stand so that we might be One?

Take for example the story of the Garden of Eden, our Fall from Grace. I ask you: Who wrote that? Do we know? Was it one person? Has the story been revised? Isn't it interesting that much of humanity hangs in the balance over this one story?

I got in deep trouble for asking those questions as a young child, but I feel the same way today as I did all those many years ago. That story, along with many others that I've heard, doesn't ring true to me—not at all. I personally know it to be wrong because of my connection to our Shared Parent.

All I'm asking is that you keep an open mind, and entertain the possibilities. Or skip the rest of this chapter if you are deeply religious and it's too much for you. I think you'll find other value in this handbook, even if you skip this chapter completely.

> *"If you resist reading what you disagree with, how will you ever acquire deeper insights into what you believe? The things most worth reading are precisely those that challenge our convictions."*
>
> *— Anonymous*

Jesus, along with the terms Christ (Greek for "anointed One") and Christ Consciousness, also needs addressing. Jesus was a man. Specifically, Jesus of Nazareth, or as I believe we should refer to him, Yeshua Ben Joseph.

Yeshua Ben Joseph was a man who remembered his connection to his Creative Parent, whom he is quoted as referring to as "the Father" or "my Father": "No one gets to the Father but through me." In that quote, he tells us that as long as we remember our connection to the same Creative Parent, we can do as he did—or even greater things! That quote has been horribly misinterpreted by some. Yeshua Ben Joseph's whole life and legacy has been twisted between poor translations, small minds, and grabs for control and power.

Yeshua Ben Joseph, as a man, achieved and demonstrated the consciousness of an anointed one; therefore, he became referred to as "The Christ." This is where the term Jesus Christ came from, and the term Christ Consciousness. These are small but important details that I believe have been lost in translation over time, and these misconceptions have helped to muddy the waters of understanding and truth.

Yeshua Ben Joseph came to this life to show us how to live a life of enlightenment so that we might experience joy, harmony, and peace. However, that is not what we have been taught; sin, guilt, and other religious burdens were never the purpose of Yeshua. He attempted to form a new way to live, based on his beliefs, that would lead us back to the lives of love and joy we are supposed to be living. When it became clear that he was to die, he went, willingly, because he knew it was his path. He understood that every moment of his life was divine because he was always connected to his Great Parent, our Shared Parent. It's the same Parent—Jesus' Parent, and your Parent, and my Parent. Christianity didn't come about because everyone worshiped Yeshua Ben Joseph for his talents and founded a religion in his honor, but in actuality, Yeshua Ben Joseph founded Christianity himself.

Yeshua Ben Joseph was just like any other self-declared messiah, with the exception that his skills outshine those of any other messiah to date. No one we know of has replicated the miracles of Yeshua Ben Joseph. Falling short of that, to embody Christ Consciousness is to attain the same level of understanding that Yeshua Ben Joseph demonstrated. And that, many agree, people have attained. Here are a few who have attained Christ Consciousness:

- St. Francis
- St. Therese of Lisieux
- St. John of the Cross
- Mahavatar Babaji
- Krishna

- Ramakrishna
- Yogananda
- Buddha

Can you think of any others?

Christ is a word to describe a state of consciousness, which was fully manifest in Yeshua Ben Joseph—and in others. It is a consciousness of our Creative or Heavenly Parent. Our Shared Parent, Our Parental Source, Our Parent.

However, the fact remains that all these words—God, Christ, Jesus, The Father—and the dogma of formalized religions—can be alienating when we try to talk about what's really happening here on Earth, in this third dimension in which we find ourselves.

Among the people working to find peace and oneness, there's an urge to talk about evolution and becoming something "new," but it's really not that at all. It's about going back to our roots; it's about reconnecting with what we really are, what we *already* are but have forgotten! It's about learning who we are, *who we really are*, from within.

A friend of mine told me that her kids ask her, "You keep telling us we came here to do something, we have a purpose. How do we know what that is?" And she said, "What do I tell them? I don't even know that for myself? No one ever tells us that: how to find our purpose. How do we figure that out?"

She's right, isn't she? We hear, "You can be anything you want," but are we given the tools to do that? (Don't worry, I am going to give them to you!)

As I mentioned, from my first moments after birth, this place confused and overwhelmed me. I had to get to the bottom of what was going on around here; I *had* to find answers. The first place I focused on was religion because religion was always something that bothered my mother, and she shared that bother with me.

Although I was very unhappy with my mother for most of my life, I have come to realize she was exactly what I needed, as I'm sure you'll see as these stories emerge. (Thank you, Mommy!)

My mother was too smart for religion. What I mean is that religion, all religion, any religion, is a compilation of numerous people's input over time. We really don't know anything about the beginning of humanity; our recorded history all starts once we developed language and writing. The Bible was written by numerous people. Whenever you have a situation such as that, you are bound to have some inconsistencies and anomalies. My mother's mind was like a trap. She would latch on to every inconsistency or fantastic recollection, and she would spend hours haranguing me with her troubles, wrapping her mind around things. I think she was either an agnostic or an atheist. I'm not sure she ever knew for herself what she was.

She wasn't willing to be responsible for my religious upbringing or lack of it, so she dragged me all over, to all kinds of different churches. We went to a Presbyterian Church in New York City, a Dutch Reformed Church, an Episcopal Church, and several others in upstate New York that I don't remember.

All the different churches were torture for me. Not a single place seemed to understand what I understood about life. Not a single person seemed to treat Jesus in a way that made sense to me. First of all, Jesus was just one of many who had a message, but his words in particular seemed to be manipulated, or at a minimum, misunderstood.

I liked the singing, but not necessarily the words of the hymns; I enjoyed the pretty windows. Sometimes, there were decent things to eat. Of all of the churches my mother took me to, I liked the Episcopal Church the best because of the richness of the church (it had great stained glass) and the rituals. I love rituals because they can be wonderful mindfulness exercises, or at least that is how I always looked at them.

The longer I went to church, though, the less I respected what I saw. I was particularly bothered by the obvious hypocrisy. I was troubled by the focus on appearances. Even as a small child (I'm talking age two, three, five), the whole business of dressing up for church bothered me. It seemed like everyone was a bunch of phonies. I didn't fail to notice that everyone behaved as he or she wanted the rest of the week. People acted nice on Sundays, but the rest of the week, look out! What a bunch of phonies, indeed!

The differences between all the churches made me curious, though. I couldn't figure out why there were so many variations. Why couldn't everyone agree? From the time I was old enough to think about these things, I became troubled. So at some point, I decided I was going to sort it out for myself. I wasn't willing to believe anyone else; I had to find the truth myself.

I started with the fractions of Christianity. That was pretty interesting since when you trace the fractions, you end up at the whole. Then I went on to Judaism, then Islam, then Hindu. Do you know what happens when you do this? Have you ever thought about all the different religions and where they came from? How about the Native American cultures? What about the African cultures? I'm here to tell you that you can start anywhere, trace it back, keep tracing it back, find where it started, how it started, what it started out saying...get all the way back to the beginning of each one. Have you ever done it? Do you have any idea what you find when you do? You have no idea how many people I've asked this question of. In not quite sixty years, five people have known the answer—where do you get when you trace any religion to its origin?

Have you guessed it yet?

You get to the *same place.*

You get to *the same* four letter word.

Love!

That's right. If you do it, you will find the same thing. You *will not* arrive at hate and misery, fear and loathing, death and despair, sickness and lack. You will find *love. Love, joy, and peace.* You will find the word or meaning of AAH. AAH and spirit have existed from the very first moments of thought in the form of language. There has always been the One Great Parent, the All That IS, the Oneness of All, the Universe, one Supreme Mind. You will find that each and every single religion starts in the concept of love and service. It's not just enough to be here and be loving; we are here to serve one another.

> *"If you focus entirely on [serving] others,*
> *the world seems to reward you the most."*
>
> *— Derek Sivers*

We all have a talent or a skill we came here to perfect and share. We are not nurtured to develop to our soul's fullest potential. We are not brought up talking about our souls at all. Not on a mass scale, certainly not as children. And as adults, rather than honoring each person's personal expression, we tend to force our children to take a shape we want them to take. We are given statements like "You came here for a reason, or with a purpose." But we're not given any guidance on how to find that purpose or fulfill it.

In my study of religion, I discovered one religion that got as close to "right" as any. The Society of Friends, or Quakers, came as close to any in its tenet that, "There is that of God in every person." The Quakers, to this day, still operate from the heart, from a place of service and respect of humanity.

Interestingly, when I ended up in foster care at age fifteen, I got to live with a family of Friends. What an amazing experience that was—to live with people who could actually begin to understand me. I was a strange child, as you may have gleaned. Because of their Friends' philosophy, for the first time in my life I felt at home; I actually felt seen for the first time. (As far as my parents were concerned, I was a bad child, until they got my IQ test results when I was ten. After that, I was just a problem child.)

I will be forever indebted to the social worker who thought to approach my foster family about me, when they were no longer in the system, and to them for saying yes.

I spent my last two years of high school attending a Friends high school where there were only eighteen girls in my graduating class. We attended Quaker Meeting every Wednesday as part of our curriculum. One hour of meditation each week—how marvelous that was. I really respect the Society of Friends for how it conducted its worship. Meeting, the Quakers' name for church, is how the Friends worship together—

in silent meditation until someone is moved by AAH within him or her to speak. There are no priests or ministers since the Friends believe that all are equal. What they do have are Elders, and in the Meeting Hall, there are Facing Benches, which is where the Elders sit. The Meeting I attended honored the youth also, so each week there were youth who were invited to sit on the Facing Benches with the Elders.

There were many meetings that were totally silent for the entire time. Since the only time anyone would speak would be when he or she was moved by AAH, you never knew what the Meeting topic might be, if any; you would just go and be, and see what happened, see what came up, either in you that you felt moved by Spirit to share, or in someone else who was moved to share.

There were some incredible times in that Meeting House—some baring of souls, some inspiration that moved us to tears, some sharing that made our hearts sing. As a teenager, I was moved to tears by my experiences, by the astounding love and openness that these people showed in their religion. At the end of each meeting, you would turn to the person next to you and shake hands. Then, of course, you would end up shaking hands with everyone around you and then gladly gathering for Social Hour in the social hall. There was food and beverages, and everyone chatted it up.

I found such peace and love there that, as a sixteen year old, I asked to become a member of the Meeting. I truly felt I had found a home. If you ever find yourself where there is a traditional Society of Friends Meeting, I encourage you to attend and experience this beautiful form of worship.

Meditation is a form of worship. That might strike a good many of you as a new thought—especially many of you who meditate. Let me explain myself. You are a divine being. It does not matter what religion you may call your own or whether you believe yourself an atheist or agnostic. You are still a divine being. What makes things real in this regard exists outside of your thoughts. Your thoughts either support or interfere with the ISness that you are.

In Section 2, I will be taking you through all of this in detail, but basically, you are not the body you see—you are much larger than that. You are an energetic being, and your energetic being is a part of a larger energetic being. Your spirit, the energy of this lifetime in the third dimension, has a purpose; you have a reason for being here. The only way to discover your reason for being here is to go inside yourself.

"...you believe lies,
so you eventually learn to trust no one but yourself...."

— Marilyn Monroe

Go within. Actually, whenever you are in doubt, do not go around asking a lot of people their opinions. Instead, go within. You will get the answers you need. The entire Universe is within you, if you go within and learn how to connect with it. I promise you this.

"When you realize nothing is lacking,
the whole world belongs to you."

— Lao Tzu

Are there times you can think of in your life when religion has caused any kind of problem, division, upset, or separation between you and others?

Can you think of five ways we can overcome the problems that religion can cause in daily life?

1)

2)

3)

4)

5)

"God has no religion."

— Mahatma Gandhi

BALANCING YOUR ROOT CHAKRA

"Our own physical body possesses a wisdom which we who inhabit the body lack. We give it orders which make no sense."

Henry Miller

Your root chakra honors the earth, and its function is to give you your life force or vitality. Balancing your root chakra will bring you into good health with a positive feeling about life and the world. Using sound as a balancing tool, you can chant LAM; if you can do it at the tone of C (261 hz), all the better! Eating red foods and also protein will help balance your root chakra. Getting a pedicure can help because your feet are your roots. You can use aroma therapy from oils coming from the root or trunk, such as juniper, frankincense, sandalwood, rosewood, cedarwood, and tea tree, and also perhaps rose (as in roses are red). Be careful with any candles or flames! Never leave a flame unattended. You can do yoga, or meditate with your forefinger and thumbs, making circles with your hand resting on your knees.

You can use some of the clearing statements mentioned earlier for your root chakra. Affirmations also work. Try saying, "I am a divine being of light, and I am peaceful, protected, and secure."

"When I dare to be powerful, to use my strength in the service of my vision, then it becomes less and less important that I am afraid."

— Andre Lorde

Chapter 7

FILLING IN THE GAPS

"There will be no end of the troubles of states, or humanity itself, till philosophers become kings in this world, or till those we now call kings and rulers really and truly become philosophers, and political power and philosophy thus come into the same hands."

— *Plato*

I hope you are still with me! The chapter you just read is likely the most challenging in the entire book to get through; if you're still with me, then we're going to become good friends, I think!

We are walking a fine line, and when we look back through the timeline, we can see we've been on this warring edge from the beginning of recorded history. We very early on in our existence slipped into the mindset of, "We'll just kill the people we disagree with or whose things we want."

There is so much more that could also be included in "setting up" our starting point together in these Halls of History, but rather than spend much more time on this, let's wrap it up so we can get on to the good stuff!

As you'll recall, a lot of philosophers are listed in the timeline. I thought of including psychologists and more scientists, but I decided enough was enough. The timeline is just to make a point. It really is true that you can likely find someone who will agree and someone else who will disagree on just about any point you can think of, from science to human development. Everyone has a theory.

> *"We have also arranged things so that almost no one understands science and technology. This is a prescription for disaster. We might get away with it for a while, but sooner or later this combustible mixture of ignorance and power is going to blow up in our faces."*
>
> *— Carl Sagan*

There are some other theories that we should at least touch upon, some additional data we should at least glance at, and a few unanswered questions we should take a look at.

One question you might have is: What is the difference between being religious and being spiritual? I think the simplest answer is, as Deepak Chopra says, "Religion is belief in someone else's experience. Spirituality is having your own experience."

This is, in fact, a fundamental and critical point. If you are religious, you have accepted the truth from others. (Unless you're one of the people starting some new denomination or religion. Then you are suggesting to others that they should embrace your truth.)

Being spiritual comes from your own experience; it leads to a larger, more indefinable understanding, that can be shared through the principles of Oneness. Ultimately, it leads to the truth of connection.

Because there is no single Spirituality or New Age leader, it is impossible to get a head count, or know how many people would truly describe themselves as spiritual first. The structure of Love By LIGHT may help solve this problem. We will go into this process in detail in Volume III, but you can visit the website (https://LoveByLIGHT.world) now for more information if you wish.

Let's go back to the beginning of life because it bears a closer look.

Life on Earth happened quite quickly by comparison to what led up to the forming of Earth. (Well, quickly when you're talking in billions of years.) It is entirely possible since life started so quickly after the formation of Earth that it could have come from elsewhere and that there is life throughout the Universe. Panspermia is the hypothesis that life exists throughout the Universe, distributed by meteoroids, asteroids, comets, planetoids, and also, by spacecraft in the form of unintended contamination by microorganisms. Panspermia is not meant to address how life began, just the method that may cause its distribution in the Universe.

There are other theories of the origin of life. Abiogenesis suggests that it "just happened." The right combination of geophysical, biological, and chemical organic compounds led to life.

One possibility is lightning, combined with the right combination of circumstances. This is my personal favorite, and the one I believe to be the most accurate since it is commonly accepted that we are "light beings." We humans are the result of lightning. The Miller-Urey experiment, reported in 1953, showed that electric sparks can generate amino acid and sugars from an atmosphere loaded with water, methane, ammonia, and hydrogen. Lightning may have played a key role in the development of life in the early days! Ultimately, it took amino acids, which were the result of a chemical reaction on Earth or came from space.

In my understanding of how things work, all of this, however any of it came to be, was a result of the ISness contemplating itself. As our Great Parent, the ISness, the One that is All, considered itself, it became a creator in physical form. There are a multitude of dimensions, and what we see in this physical realm is a result of our contemplation and manipulation of the different dimensions. (We'll get into this concept in more detail in Section II.)

Another topic we'll get into in Section II is time.... I built a "timeline" for you, when in reality, there is no such thing as time.... But because a linear approach is necessary to see and track events, we're going to save the in-depth discussion of time for a later chapter in this volume.

Looking at events in a linear way, my understanding is that in the beginning, things happened so slowly because we had just started thinking about these things. And once we (the great ISness that we are a part of) got the hang of it, the creation of things started to happen more rapidly. Figuring out this third dimension in which we are creating was a challenge in and of itself, and it took a bit of thinking! My head hurts just thinking about the thinking we had to do to make the third dimension!

When I was doing my metaphysical work back in the 1980s-90s, the telekinesis work made my head hurt the most.

I did achieve moving a piece of paper and also a pencil on a table using just my mind, but that's a different story; let's not get off track.

Another point worth a brief mention: It is estimated that a million years ago, we developed different skin and hair colors and we began to lose our body hair. There are lots of ideas about all of this, but no one really knows anything about it. What we think is that we all supposedly started out as dark-skinned, dark-haired, and dark-eyed, and then at some point, around a million years ago, our skin lightened in color, and we developed different hair colors. The generally accepted idea is that these changes occurred due to migrating to colder climates, which makes no sense to me. What makes sense to me is that we, the One Mind, decided to try something different. Note: We didn't try different eye colors, in particular blue eyes, till just 100,000 years or so.

There's a beautiful map that shows our skin color distribution across the globe at https://whyevolutionistrue.wordpress.com/2010/07/20/why-does-skin-color-vary-among-human-populations/ Please check it out for yourself.

We have been taught that the land masses were once all connected and that something happened that caused them to drift apart. We're taught that the split occurred between the Americas and Europe/Africa. Visually, if you look at a world map, it's an easy sell because the pieces look as if they fit together. Yet, when you look at the color distribution maps of pre-humans and humans, they tell us a different story. The only thing that makes any sense, in light of the maps of color distribution, is that Australia and New Zealand were originally attached to Africa, and the Americas were attached to the eastern side of Asia. Now, suddenly, the color distribution has some cohesion. Otherwise, if you imagine the Americas nestling up to Africa and Europe, the color distribution between South America and Africa makes no sense at all.

(There are contradictory maps out there that would match up with the popular plate tectonics story, as can be predicted. I raise the subject just as a question and suggest you draw your own conclusions.)

However, maps of how language developed match the theory that the plates of land separated in the Pacific region, not the Atlantic. Language distribution maps show human migration as if the continents were joined in the reverse of what we've been told.

Noam Chomsky, a prominent proponent of discontinuity theory, argues that a single chance mutation occurred in one individual about 100,000 years ago, instantaneously installing the language faculty in perfect or near-perfect form. It follows from this theory that language appeared rather suddenly within the history of human evolution.

As we touched upon earlier, our closest cousins are chimpanzees—we share 98.8 percent of their DNA. What scientists now know is that there are two distinct lines of chimpanzees—common and bonobo. We are equally related to both.

Common chimpanzees do not like strangers at all, and they are known for raping, killing, and warring; their current population numbers are thriving. Bonobo chimpanzees, on the other hand, have never been known to kill anything—and they are almost extinct.

It's so interesting, and if you buy into the theory of evolution, it's a little confusing, isn't it? That the loving chimps are almost extinct? We put a lot of value in Darwin's theory of evolution and survival of the fittest. Why aren't the loving chimps the fittest? Is it our genetics that make us violent? Is that the root of our problems with creating the Heaven on Earth we came here to create? Dr. Bruce Lipton, in his book *The Biology of Belief*, tells us we can change our genetics by changing our beliefs.

Or is it, as some suggest, that our troubles really started with the development of language? With it came the ability to deceive, to misrepresent, and to lie.

Noam Chomsky theorizes the start of language was a sort of leap in our evolution—caused by a mutation. It causes me to pause and wonder: What if this mutation were an aha! moment in the process of creation? We figured out how we needed to modify the chimpanzee jaw and mouth structure to make more controllable sounds...so what if in our creation, we decided to try it in one creation, and to mark the creation with blue eyes, so we could keep track of the progress easily?

The two mutations (the development of language and the first appearance of blue eyes) are said to have occurred 100,000 years ago. What if these two mutations happened at the same time, in the same single human? It seems too coincidental that there would be two world-changing mutations at the same time. There are no coincidences. It's interesting, isn't it? Fascinating, but actually not important overall—as I will show you in Section 2. Before we get there, let's take a moment to look at language a little more closely since it is likely that the development of language is when most of our troubles started. Prior to that point, it is presumed that we lived in harmony with nature. It is really not clear when or why we went from living in harmony to living in fear—to fighting and warring.

To me, why we changed and when we lost our peace and harmony, when we lost our happiness, is a critical moment to understand. It became incredibly important to me that I figure this out. Just as I had to trace the religions to find the truth, I had to figure this out.

If we stop to consider how this evolution of humanity occurred, it seems that it likely went something like this: We used sign language first, along with sounds. Eventually, we drew pictures, we perfected our sounds, and in time, we made a connection between sounds and drawings. Did this occur when we came together with a different group of humans? Or did we start writing things down as a way to keep records, either for business or history? No one really knows.

If you have ever watched children of different languages play together, you'll see they instantly overcome their barriers. They figure out a way to communicate. When I was a small child, we lived in Beirut, Lebanon. There were many English-speaking children, but the daughter of our housekeeper was my age, and we played together our entire lives until I moved away. She spoke Arabic. It never mattered. Jacqueline and I would play for hours, and we never suffered from a language barrier.

It is my impression that the development of language is responsible for the first lies being told. The Bible would have us believe the first lie was the serpent speaking to Adam and Eve in the Garden of Eden. Yet the Bible itself, in the telling of the story, tells the first lie because Adam and Eve did not die that day. So in the most published book on Planet Earth, we can't get out of Chapter 1 (Genesis) without confusion about what is true or what the first lie was.

We could ask *when*, but really, the more important question is *why* did we as humans decide we needed to lie to each other? Why did we need to use language to deceive each other?

St. Augustine identified eight kinds of lies:

1. Lies in religious teachings
2. Lies that harm others and help no one
3. Lies that harm others and help someone
4. Lies told for the pleasure of lying
5. Lies told to "please others during conversation"
6. Lies that harm no one yet help someone
7. Lies that harm no one and save life
8. Lies that harm no one and save someone's "purity"

Consider how many synonyms there can be for a lie: ambiguity, bluff, fabrication, falsehood, falsity, fib, mendacious, prevarication, story, tale, untruth, whopper, tarradiddle, distortion, exaggeration, obliquity, misreport, deceit, duplicity, fraud, hoax, jest, omission, perjury, propaganda, etc.

I ask you to think hard about this because I believe it is one of the real keys to understanding how we can fix things now. It's also a key to where, when, and why things went so awry and made Heaven on Earth appear so elusive. At some point in our evolution, something happened so that we could no longer just co-exist. Something happened to make us distrustful and deceitful, and from that moment, our troubles began.

The root of the word "war" is "worse"—to make worse. I heard someone say recently that the original usage was "to confuse," as in the enemy. In any event, when did that start, our need to confuse and make worse for others, and why? How do we stop the warring and make peace?

Life on Planet Earth in the twenty-first century is extremely challenging. The 7 billion plus humans on this planet are really struggling. Regardless of the reasons why, one can't ignore the climate changes affecting everyone—raising ocean/sea levels, a decline in breathable air, a decline in drinkable water, an increase in earthquakes, and a shift in weather patterns that is resulting in extremes of all kinds, causing loss of life and property around the globe.

Socially, fear has gripped the planet to a degree that is of greatest concern. The United States, founded on equality and love, has sunk to a low that can't be captured in these pages. What is being played out in the political arena can't be put into words; you just have to live through it to understand—and there's no understanding even then. In the late 2010s, a certain lunacy permeates the airwaves. It is easy to say that democracy for many has been lost to an oligarchy. Money, greed, and the lust for power has taken over the world—even religion has been lost to it.

Enough conspiracy theories exist to make your head spin. As I've mentioned, I witnessed one huge media conspiracy, so there is no doubt in my mind that conspiracy exists at a level we can't wrap our heads around. I lived through JFK's assassination. Hanging chads were a conspiracy. We're living through the conspiracy of the Republican-held U.S. Senate as I write this. Books have been written on the subject of conspiracies; surely some of them have merit.

I wouldn't be filling in the gaps without a mention of both the occult and aliens. Neither of these are things I encourage pursuing. As we know, everything is energy. My personal philosophy is to keep your energy at home. Leave the energy of the occult and aliens to themselves. I was fascinated to learn from Chris Goode that the aliens he has worked with only want us to be more loving, more forgiving, and more helpful to others. Great to know we're working toward a common goal!

While both of these things exist (aliens and the occult), I am here to show you that what really matters is what we think about, and that the most important thing we can think about is ourselves and our spirit and soul's purpose. Whenever we are thinking of anything other than our joy and loving everything, we are stalled in our evolution. We do not realize we are disconnected from our Source, disconnected from our personal power, disconnected from our wisdom, and disconnected from our souls.

I am here to light the path back to reconnection with yourself, and what brings you joy and peace, which will result in a world of peace and joy.

What strikes you most about this chapter? Have you had the experience of spirituality? How do you feel about the eight kinds of lies? Do you have a sense of when humankind's troubles began?

1)

2)

3)

4)

5)

"If we could unfold the future,
the present would be our greatest care."
— Edward Counsel

STRENGTHENING YOUR ROOTS
ROOT CHAKRA

"To be rooted is perhaps the most important and least recognized need of the human soul."

— Simone Weil

The symbol/element of the root chakra is Earth. When you have a healthy root chakra, you will feel secure and as if you have your legs under you. You will feel firmly planted. You will feel safe. You will enjoy good health and energy and happiness in your job and finances. You will be of good proportional weight and physically fit, with a good sense of wellbeing and satisfaction in life. You will feel grounded and settled, centered and strong. It will be easy for you to let go of things no longer needed, and you will enjoy a feeling of security and safety.

The root chakra core wound is fear, and it rules your legs and feet, your immune system, and kidneys. It governs everything in your lower region, including: bowels, buttock, large intestine. It also rules your teeth and bones (the roots of your body), eating disorders, and frequent illness.

If you have issues with your root chakra, blockages, then you may suffer from things like chronic illness, persistent and repetitive medical experiences, problems with breaking bones or rotting teeth, and chronic indigestion.

"Get yourself grounded and you can navigate even the stormiest roads in peace."

— Steve Goodier

All of these maladies are the result of a core fear. Here are some clearing statements to help strengthen your root chakra:

- "I release and let go of everything that I am afraid of."
- "I release and let go of my fears of abandonment."
- "I release and let go of my feelings of persecution."
- "I release and let go of my fears of inadequacy."

Here are some affirmations:

- "I am safe and secure, and I have everything I need."
- "I am stable and steady and can easily navigate life's path."
- "I am strong and able."
- "I am respected and loved."
- "I matter."
- "I am important."
- "I am worthy."
- "I matter, and I am worthy and important."

"And remember, no matter where you go, there you are."

— Confucius

Chapter 8

REWRITING HISTORY

"One of the saddest lessons of history is this: If we've been bamboozled long enough, we tend to reject any evidence of the bamboozle. We're no longer interested in finding out the truth. The bamboozle has captured us. It's simply too painful to acknowledge, even to ourselves, that we've been taken. Once you give a charlatan power over you, you almost never get it back."

— Carl Sagan

So here we are, near the end of the first section of *Walking Through Your Walls*. In these past chapters, I've dragged you through a lot of information. I hope you're still with me!

To sum things up, it's fair to say that at this point, religion doesn't seem able to solve the problems of the world, nor does wealth, nor does science, nor do the drug companies, in spite of their culture of "There's a pill for that."

Many people out in the world right now are suggesting we need something new. Millions of people are seeking a "new world," or at least a new experience of the world we have. What I would suggest is that we already have, and have always had, everything we ever needed, right here, right now, within us. We are all powerful beyond our wildest dreams. You are more powerful than you can imagine. If you don't feel powerful, you are not alone, not by any means. There's a myriad of reasons why you feel powerless, and I intend to illuminate the way for you to get your power back.

An awakening is occurring on this planet in the hearts and minds of humanity. In actuality, it is really more of a combined remembering of our roots and a forgetting of the illusions of this third dimension. Many are calling this an evolution into a New Human or Super Human. What I see is more of a reclaiming of our birthrights and talents and a reconnecting with our internal guidance systems. It is possible that as we awaken and reconnect, we are genetically changing, and by so doing, we are evolving.

In order for us to achieve the ability to create a new world, we are going to have to "wipe the film clean," as Edward Mannix would say. Each of us has been imprinted with everything we have experienced in this realm. In Volume II, I'll go into more details on how to wipe the film clean at an individual level, but for the moment, let's look at what we can do at a broader level, at the level of humanity.

As we have seen, the truth, is elusive.

"History is always written by the winners. When two cultures clash, the loser is obliterated, and the winner writes the history books—books which glorify their own cause and disparage the conquered foe."

— Dan Brown

History is constantly being rewritten. Governments rewrite history as they decide what they want the people to be told. Certainly, it would appear that scientists are at the helm of this movement nowadays. As they perfect their tools, they achieve an accuracy previously unknown and, thereby, can re-date, re-calibrate, re-analyze, etc. As we saw earlier, for years and years we've been told that Homo sapiens came from Africa, but we now think they come from Australia. What else have we gotten wrong? Perhaps everything!

Another thing I hope I've shown you is that lots and lots of people have had theories about something, and many of those theories have been popular for a while and then lost popularity, or are so popular that they get repeated and reinterpreted to the degree that the original message gets lost in translation or over-interpretation. In essence, whenever we are looking outside ourselves at theory, we are lost. Everyone has a theory, but no one yet has gotten it totally right—and I don't suppose I am getting it 100 percent right either. All I can say is that I've experienced all that I write about, and it feels true. If it didn't feel true, I wouldn't be sharing it with you.

What if I were further to suggest that by rewriting our history, we might heal all the emotional wounds we've been carrying with us as a result of the old story? Doesn't it follow that you might need to be open to a new story if you would like your life to unfold with the power of your Creative Parent and the Universe?

Below I am going to tell you what I believe is the true story of what happened on that first day when the Great One Mind, the All That IS, AAH, thought Adam and Eve into creation.

Here's the gift a New Story of the Garden of Eden gives us. By telling it, we are going back on our "film" to our beginning of time imprint, and we are making a new imprint. We are *allowing* this new story to have a creation. All that exists is a thinking, feeling substance, and by changing our beliefs, everything around us will feel the shift, as each of us embraces this New Story of Eden, and in that feeling, we will reflect in return the new, uplifted happiness of the story. Everything around us will be so happy, and the happiness of what surrounds us will loop back to help make us happy! (How this works will be explained in Section 2 and in great detail in Volume II.)

The New Story of The Garden of Eden....

> Once upon a time, the Great One Mind, AAH, was contemplating this magnificent jewel of a planet that the Mind had created, and it further contemplated how to be able to experience the extraordinary bliss that was so apparent upon it. AAH had already spent a fair amount of contemplation time decorating the planet with all kinds of different plants and flowers, and lots of other life: birds, mammals, reptiles, etc. A true abundance, and more were coming, as the Mind (we) would think of a new design. Our creative force was quite amazing, and our imagination was unlimited. (It still is—we just don't realize it.)
>
> So AAH created two humans, deciding that allowing those two to make the next humans would be a really fun thing to experience. We had experienced childbirth in other species, but these humans, they seemed

really ideal for experiencing the bliss and beauty of life. We, AAH, had spent some time contemplating this. We had been making adjustments to our design until we'd reached what seemed like perfection.

Now, in the course of AAH's creation of Earth, a few glitches happened. As hard as one might contemplate something, when building or experimenting, there can be unintended results. So when AAH placed Eve and Adam on the Paradise of Earth, or Eden, as AAH called it, the following was communicated to Adam and Eve:

"This is Eden, on Gaia (Earth as we call it). It is a paradise beyond anything we have created so far! You should be able to live happily and comfortably, and everything around you is supporting you. There is plenty to eat and build shelter from—everything you need."

What the Great One Mind Thought is, "This is going to be *so much* fun!"

It was the original reality game, if you will. Then, almost as an afterthought:

"Oh, say, I almost forgot! I had made you a Garden so you would have everything you need quite handy, but for some reason, something didn't quite go right in there. I thought it would just be easy for you always to have a place that would just magically produce food for you, without having to go through the cycles we've created in life. Not sure what went wrong, but just ignore the Garden and especially the large tree in the middle. We experimented with cloning, but it didn't work. There are some animals in the garden that didn't turn out quite as imagined; no worries, they can't get out. But just to be on the safe side, stay out of there. The rest of Eden (the planet Gaia, or Earth) is fair game—go forth, explore, enjoy!"

So Eve and Adam take up life on Eden. Before heading off that first day of creation, they dragged some branches and rolled a few rocks in front of the entrance to the Garden, just to make sure they never accidentally ended up in the Garden. They intended to honor their Parent's request.

They lived happily and they stayed away from the Garden and life was magnificent. Then one day while out hiking, they happened upon the entrance to the Garden. When they realized they had almost entered the Garden because the things they had blocked the entrance with had deteriorated, Adam suggested that Eve go off and gather them some lunch while he stayed to re-block the Garden's entrance.

When Eve returned, she was shocked to see the Garden's entrance still open and Adam inside! She dropped the fruit she was carrying and ran to the entrance. "Adam! Adam! What are you doing?" she asked. Adam came to the entrance, clearly a little confused or intoxicated, holding an apple, with the snake wrapped around his forearm, charming him.

"Oh, hey, Eve! Look at who I met!" said Adam. "This lovely talking snake; can you believe it? You know, he was telling me there's no need to wander around all the time—we could move in here where the food just magically appears!"

Eve, realizing that the energy inside the Garden was really strange, and of course, remembering the warning of her Parent, AAH, instantly knew Adam was in trouble. She knew she was his counterpart and was here to be with him through thick and thin, to stand by him, if you will. (It was, after all, just the two of them. There was no survival or future alone.)

She knew she could not support Adam in this case, however, nor should she. Instead, she knew she had to invoke her knowledge about their bodies and about healing. She knew that Adam's Crown Chakra had become blocked; that he had disconnected from AAH in part, if not totally, and that he was being influenced only by the physical third-dimension gravity. It was, after all, what was keeping them from flying off into space. Gravity was one of the last things AAH created before we created life. Without it, life would have been impossible since everything was ending up spread across the galaxies. That was actually quite the mess for AAH to clean up!

So what to do—what to do? Eve realized there was only one thing she could do!

"Adam, sweetheart, can you step outside the Garden, just for a minute? I don't want to waste this fruit since I picked it!"

When Adam came out (without the snake, since the snake was confined to the Garden by design), Eve swiftly walked up to Adam, hugged him, and whispered in his ear: "You will forgive me this once it is over and you are back to your senses."

She stepped away from him and looked him straight in the eye. "Ready?"

Adam cocked his head in wonder. Eve grabbed Adam and put him in a headlock and gave him a brisk and thorough noogie!

"There, I just reopened your crown chakra. Let's give it a few seconds to reconnect with Source. Then I expect you'll be anxious to close that entrance to the Garden and your buddy, the snake!"

Adam stood there for a few moments, the top of his head burning and smarting from the noogie, and then the tingling subsided and he realized that his breathing, which had become quite shallow while in the Garden, had sunk again into his lower belly. Suddenly, all the color drained out of his face.

"What happened?" he cried.

"You were cozied up to the snake when I got back from picking fruit. He must have charmed you into the Garden."

"Let's finish what I was supposed to start! And then let's go; let's go as far away from here as we can so we never come back," said Adam.

This time, Eve and Adam found some really large rocks and totally blocked the entrance to the Garden with them. They worked for a few days blocking the entrance. Even though it was just the two of them, they knew in the future there would be others—it was important that no one ever enter the Garden.

Finally, when they were done, Eve turned to Adam and said, "Now we can go off and live the great experience of humanity experiencing heaven on Earth! Good thing we didn't let all of history down by screwing up first thing!"

And with that, they wrapped their arms around each other in total, infinite, unconditional, and unending love and went off to complete the story.

And they all lived happily ever after.

I ask you to stay in that world for a moment or two longer and imagine, if you will, the future from that point forward, instead of as the classic story goes. No fall from grace—no sin. Wouldn't you like to live in *that* world instead? Do you know how simple it is? It's as simple as this: Believe *this* story.

Are there things about your history you would like to rewrite? How might your life be different had you made different choices? How would the world be different without the story of original sin?

1)

2)

3)

4)

5)

"He who controls the past controls the future.
He who controls the present controls the past."

— George Orwell

SUMMARIZING THE HALLS OF HISTORY

"If you don't know history, then you don't know anything. You are a leaf that doesn't know it is part of a tree."

— Michael Crichton

We've covered a lot of ground together. If you've skipped ahead because the details don't interest you, I can't blame you a bit! Many of the details didn't interest me, but if my role or assignment is to shine a light on things, then we needed to go into those details. You can always go back and find what you need, if it turns out there's something you missed. It's a handbook, so it seems reasonable you might jump around in it.

As we prepare to enter the maze of walls together, I want to thank you for taking this journey of exploration with me. I hope I have illuminated things you have not yet noticed, and that if you have had questions, you've reached out to me via Facebook or one of the other methods outlined in the Introduction and About the Author sections.

What does history mean really? It means only what we believe it to mean. It means only what others believe it to be. It means it's the edited truth; somebody is responsible for deciding each truth you've been taught, but how true was the truth you were told?

It will be interesting to see how history will unveil itself in the coming months and years. Truth has become more and more elusive. Recent revelations of deep corruption around the world are shattering some of the myths of the current history books. Will capitalism continue to rule? Will the powers that be continue to ignore the clear signs of climate change? Will the people of Earth be so gullible as to be hoodwinked into the oligarchy's lies? What will the history books say in fifty years? The future of the planet hangs in the balance, awaiting our awakening.

"Vision without action is merely a dream. Action without vision just passes time. Vision with action can change the world."

— Joel A. Barker

SECTION 2

THE WALLS OF LIFE

"That's the key to walking through the Wall....
You have to first see it as not being a Wall,
even though everyone you know still sees it as a Wall."

— Kevin J. Shay

Chapter 1

FINDING YOUR I AM PRESENCE

"Very little is needed to make a happy life; it is all within yourself, in your way of thinking."

— Marcus Aurelius

I am here to shine a light on all the confusion, and in so doing un-bamboozle you; I am here to help you find your power and get it back. As Carl Sagan says, "Once you give a charlatan power over you, you almost never get it back." A lot has gone into disempowering us; it's time to find our way home to our source. It's time each one of us connect to our spirit and live our lives fulfilling our spirit and soul's purpose.

In Section I, we looked at where you and I find ourselves, on Earth/Gaia/Eden, and how we got here, according to the history books—and you know what I think of them!

What I am going to do now is break down what I see are the walls that keep us from understanding life in a way that allows us to participate in our experiences to the highest vibration possible and always get the best outcome. If we were vibrating at our highest frequencies, you and I would be able to walk through walls, walk on water, and a whole lot more—but these things have to be done in all seriousness and with purpose, not merely for show or experiment.

In life, we are instantly at a disadvantage. As illustrated and illuminated in the Halls of History section, what we've been taught has been decided for us by people in power and with money. The walls that loom are ignored, and we are encouraged to wander blindly through life listening to the rich and powerful. We are taught to become what those around us tell us to become. We are told to believe what we are being told.

Don't you think you deserve the truth—the unadulterated truth—so you can decide for yourself what's important to you? What's relevant to you? It is my hope that this handbook gives you the truth you need to live an educated, whole, authentic, and genuinely awakened life.

"There are four kinds of people in the world, Ms. Harper. Those who build walls. Those who protect walls. Those who breach walls. And those who tear down walls. Much of life is discovering who you are. When you find out, you also realize there are places you can no longer go, things you can no longer do, words you can no longer say."

— P.S. Baber, Cassie Draws the Universe

You deserve to be educated about the things you really need to know, to maximize the power within you, to allow you to find wholeness and authenticity. You are a magnificent being, capable of astounding things. You can walk on water. You can physically walk through walls. You can time travel. You are a creator and capable of magnificent manifestations. Your body can be whole and without pain. You can live comfortably in your meat suit, and you can heal from anything. You deserve to live your genuine life!

You're shaking your head aren't you? Wall #1.

Are you living the life of your dreams? Are you always happy, regardless of circumstances? Do you find it easy to stay on center, in touch with your spirit? Are you healthy?

My guess is most of you answered "No." You're likely not living the life of your spirit or dreams—likely not happy regardless of circumstances. There is a good chance you are not healthy, even though you try to be. Am I right? Why aren't you happy? Why aren't you healthy? Whose job is it to make you happy and healthy? Volumes II and III go into these concepts in great detail.

For now, to a great extent, and for our purposes here, let me say: We tend to live the lives we're told to live. We live the lives we're expected to live, by others. We live the lives in front of us. We take one step after the other, and we don't really question where we're led or where we end up (until we end up there). We follow the impulses of our body.

> *"Your work is going to fill a large part of life, and the only way to be truly satisfied is to do what you believe is great work. And the only way to do great work is to love what you do. If you haven't found it yet, keep looking. Don't settle. As with all matters of the heart, you'll know when you find it."*
>
> *— Steve Jobs*

If you're connected to your Great One Parent, if you're connected to AAH, if you're connected to your joy, then you're on the path of your spirit's assignment and your soul's purpose in this lifetime. You've discovered your I AM presence and connected to it. I think you will likely still find value in this volume of the handbook, but you've made great headway already! Bravo for having the courage and persistence to do your inner work.

If you're just living life, not living a life you adore and love, not feeling joy constantly, not bathed in gratitude, not crazy giddy over the miracle that is life and the amazing experience, the amazing story, the fascinating game that it is—if you are not even thinking about it—one thing you can be assured of is that you will likely return to the third dimension in other lives to live it again, and again if necessary, to get another chance to figure it out. You came here to be happy. It is true, I believe, that we get to keep trying until we finally learn.

One reason why we live this way, in separation consciousness, perhaps, is that no one has ever pointed out that we are separated or told us how not to live this way. Sure, there are all the other walls, but this wall is the wall of "Who am I?" The most I was ever told is, "You'll figure it out."

How do we navigate life? How do we figure out who we are? We look to our parents for answers, but often, our parents will tell us they don't know. Quite often when we look around, we see mundane life—people living in the same neighborhoods generation after generation. While this may appear unexciting and boring, or meaningless, in a later section you'll see how this is a magnificent display of an energetic vortex, as I like to call it. People are stuck in energetic loopbacks.

After looking to our parents for answers about life, many of us will try turning to religion to tell us about life. There's so much more to understanding life than can be learned through religion. Religion can't connect you with your individual Spirit; your parents can't; your friends, teachers, coaches, doctors, priests, ministers, rabbis, etc. can't. Only you can discover who you are, who your I AM Presence is.

Every single one of us on Earth has an I AM Presence. I don't remember anyone ever telling me anything about it when I was little. I had to find it for myself. It wasn't until I was in college, taking psychology classes, that I heard about it in conversation, but I'd gotten a jumpstart on everyone without realizing it.

When I was eight or nine, my mother let me wear her sorority ring from college. It was a pinky ring for her, but I wore it on one of my middle fingers. (Even then I think I had to put some tape on it to make it fit.) It was inscribed with the René Descartes' quote in Latin, "Cogito Ergo Sum"—"I think, therefore I AM."

Yup, that was me—a little nine year old wandering the woods with her dog, thinking about "I think, therefore I AM." I didn't understand it, but I knew it was really important. I knew it was like a secret.

To a great extent, this handbook is about revealing the secrets of life.

Manipulation of history, however, has turned the tools into secrets. I want to help you make the transition to the life you love to wake up to each day. You can be in what you currently would term hell and still wake up, as I am suggesting, giddy, alive, and in love with the experience. And you will find, as you do this, your life will miraculously change.... There is a science to life, and once you understand it, life works for you. Remember, the underlying principle in all that I write about presumes an attitude of "for the good of the whole." Life does not serve those who try to manipulate life in one's personal favor. Sure, you may get what you think you want by working really hard, but when you are connected to the flow of life, you get what you want and it happens naturaly with ease.

Your ego is the construct of who you are in your mind. You are really energy with consciousness. You are not your mind. You are your thoughts. Your mind is not your thoughts. You, not your mind, are in charge of your thoughts. Ideally, you are in charge of you, rather than your ego; however, your ego thinks it is in charge. Volume II will give you lots of ways to take charge of you. In the meantime, to function in a third-dimensional realm, you need an identity, so your mind has constructed your identity—that is what your ego is.

Your *ego* thinks that it is *you* and that it's in charge!

Your ego is a set of core beliefs (self-definitions) that also serve as a defense/protection mechanism. Your ego is the mason of the wall of yourself; it has crafted walls to protect you from anything your ego has determined has, or can, hurt you. The function of the ego is to protect you, so it has protected you by constructing walls through which you cannot see. (This isn't where all the walls come from, but it's a start.)

Your ego is under the impression that there is something to fear here on Earth in this third-dimensional realm. So it creates defenses. To walk through the wall of your ego, you need to realize that your ego, and the identity of you it has created, is something your mind thought up—it's not the essence of you.

"If you want to reach a state of bliss, then go beyond your ego and the internal dialogue you are having with yourself. Make a decision to relinquish the need to control, the need to be approved, and the need to judge. Those are the three things the ego is doing all the time. It's very important to be aware of them, every time they come up."

— Deepak Chopra

You have to understand this wall is an illusion, just like everything in this third-dimensional realm is an illusion—just like all the other walls we're going to walk through.

Because your ego is involved, this is apt to be the most difficult wall to walk through. Your ego will fight you. It will not want to lose control. Just as it is your ego when you attempt to meditate that will make you want to scratch, sneeze, move, etc. It is fighting for control. When you attempt to silence your mind, you are putting your ego to bed; it will act like an angry child who does not want to go. It will raise hell. And just like with a temperamental child, we must partake in tough love and hold our ground; as with a child, it gets easier and easier, and eventually, the temperamental behavior is extinguished, and your ego learns it must relinquish control.

You need to remember that your ego serves a good function; it is just misguided. It is programming you for how it thinks you should be, instead of you programming it consciously. You can leverage your ego to your favor, which we'll talk about in Volume II.

"The ego attempts to confirm whatever and whoever you declare yourself to be, from 'I AM depressed and in debt' to 'I AM happy and free.' In order to accomplish the task of

verifying your beliefs, your ego will use any event and way of interpreting the event it finds necessary."

— Howard Falco

Trust me; you can do this. You can learn to control your ego. You can get out of your own way—and once you do, the bounty of the Universe will shower you.

One of the great things we have here on Earth/Gaia/Eden is our eyes. Our eyes bring us much joy; they show us the beauty of nature (is there anything more beautiful?); they show us our family, our spouses, our children, our grandchildren, great-grandchildren—they show us our pets, our surroundings, etc.

In the coming chapters, we will take a look at the illusion of reality: everything is moving, spinning, vibrating, and there is more space than anything solid. If everything is more space than anything and moving, what exactly IS this place? What are we seeing? Touching? Tasting? What are we? What do we mean when we say "I"?

Let's start with what we see.

What we see are light waves. All light is the vibration of the electromagnetic field. What we see then, in one sense, is the electromagnetic field. This field is made up of a variety of light waves from y-waves, X-rays, ultraviolet waves, infrared rays, micro waves, radio waves (FM, AM), and long radio waves. What we can see is a very narrow spectrum between ultraviolet and infrared, and none of those waves has any color! So when you look at a person wearing blue jeans and a green shirt, those colors are in your head. In fact, everything you see is really in your head, a movie your consciousness is creating.

You'd be amazed at what we can actually see! According to Buckminster Fuller, "Everything we see is inside our own heads." There's a great graphic of what we can see in this third-dimensional, physical realm at: http://thespiritscience.net/wp-content/uploads/2014/11/1fYGP.jpg; there's also a copy on the book website in the references section.

You are the observer, watching your creation of yourself in your head. Shift your focus away from what you are looking at, to the you who is doing the looking and *voila*! You have a whole new perspective! You can see yourself seeing others.

Once you realize you are energy—just energy—you begin truly to see. Everything else is an illusion. Energy is all there is. This is the end of all your suffering! It's the end of all human suffering!

Science has shown us that if we look at anything under the strongest microscope we have, it looks the same as anything else. Everything looks the same at the smallest level. What does that mean? There's only one thing it can mean, as far as I can see. It means that everything is made of the same stuff, fundamentally.

Oneness is not just because we are all connected. Oneness is because we are all made of the same stuff! We are one at the microscopic level. We *are* all one, one substance! Of what we see in the apparent physical world in which we live, we know that only 1 percent is actually matter.

All suffering is the result of your illusion that you are some kind of individual being, that your being exists in some form and shape in the environment, and that you need to work to survive, as your being—that your specific collection of a thousand trillion trillion atoms has to hold itself together; that you are in charge of this being, and that you must keep it safe and alive until it dies.

When you realize you are energy, all energy, just energy, and that your body is a temporary manifestation of that energy in a seemingly physical form, and when you realize that the energy you are a part of is the energy of the One Great Mind, a part of the All That IS, then you have all you need to accept that the body's death is illusionary, and death of the I AM presence that is you is something that never happens. You always are and always will *be*! As everyone else will always be. We are all simply fractions of the larger whole, in physical expression.

Your I AM lives evermore. There is nothing to be afraid of. There is no death, only the appearance of death. There is no suffering, sickness, or diseases, only the appearance of suffering and the like. There is no lack, only the appearance (and belief!) of lack. There is no evil, only the appearance of evil (the "evil" are merely your confused sisters and brothers).

You are not your mind; you exist outside of your mind. You are not your body; you exist outside of your body. You are not the image you hold in your head of yourself; you exist outside of any image.

What are some things that come to mind when you consider your I AM Presence? How do you feel when you consider your I AM Presence? Can you comfortably say, "I am the expression of all life, in physical form?"

1)

2)

3)

4)

5)

"I am in you and you in me, mutual in divine love."

— William Blake

MOVING THROUGH YOUR SACRAL CHAKRA

"Let's not forget that the little emotions are the great captains of our lives and we obey them without realizing it."

— *Vincent Van Gogh*

The second chakra is known as the sacral or spleen chakra. It is the distributor of the life force that comes from the sun, and it sends energy out to your entire body. Its motto is "I am life."

The sacral chakra is located near the lower section of your stomach, about two fingers below your navel. It rules reproduction of the physical body, creativity, joy, and relationships of the emotional body, and it rules our energy and the passions of the spiritual body. This chakra rules your adrenal glands, liver, and upper intestines, along with your reproductive organs, pancreas, and stomach. It is your emotional center, in charge of your self-gratification.

Take some time to tune into your sacral chakra, and feel into this important energy center. Focus on your breath, and continue the visualization that you started in the root chakra section, seeing the energy flowing up from the root chakra to the sacral, and then moving onward, up, around, down, up, around, down, and then up again, in a repeating toroidal pattern.

Use the following questions to access your sacral chakra:

- What do you find attractive? What repels or repulses you? How do your feelings about these things guide how you live your life?
- How attractive do you feel?
- Do you feel comfortable in your body? Are you confi-

dent about your self-image? Or do you doubt yourself often?

- Are you ruled by your emotions, or are you balanced and conscious, mindful?
- Are you overly indulgent? Do you lose balance and perspective easily? Or are you able to enjoy the special pleasures of life through moderation that comes to you easily?
- Are you able to balance passion and personal discipline?
- Do you feel expressed in your passion for life?
- Do you feel alive right now? Most of the time? Or does life feel dull to you?

Use these clearing statements to help open up your sacral chakra:

- "I release and let go of any and every thing that is keeping me from feeling and knowing that I deserve pleasure in my life."
- "I release and let go of any and every thing that is keeping me from feeling that I am safe and can feel my feelings in safety."
- "I release and let go of any and every thing that is keeping me from feeling comfortable in my sexuality."

"Trust only movement. Life happens at the level of events, not of words. Trust movement."

— Alfred Adler

Chapter 2

DEALING IN DIMENSIONS

"If quantum mechanics hasn't profoundly shocked you, you haven't understood it yet. Everything we call real is made of things that cannot be regarded as real."

— Niels Bohr

In Section 1, we discussed what constitutes the truth, we took a stroll through the history books, we took a look at the influence of religion, and we looked at some of the overall challenges humankind faces in the twenty-first century. We ended the section by rewriting history and starting humanity off on the right foot in paradise, as was intended. In Chapter 1 of this section, we walked through our wall of ego to find our self.

The entirety of this handbook (Volumes I, II, and III) is dedicated to illuminating the way back to that moment in time when our selves were one with our Great Parent, a manifestation of love, and in peace and harmony with Earth/Gaia/Eden.

Let's move on to more Walls, the first step in the process of walking ourselves home.

"Your perspective on life comes from the cage you were held captive in."

— Shannon L. Alder

The Walls are what I call all the things that keep us from realizing what is really going on here in this third-dimensional realm on Earth/Gaia/Eden. These walls are not unlike the maze pictured on the cover—it's a little hard, once inside the maze, to figure out which wall to walk through first! It's all related, all One, if you will, so in a way, we can likely start anywhere.

Let's take a look at what we know about dimensions in order to walk through the wall of density in this third dimension. This is a great place to start, the third dimension, since it is where we appear at the moment. There are numerous ways to look at dimensions and many different theories about them. Imagine! I'll review the two that make the most sense to me and are easiest to understand.

"A mind that is stretched by a new experience can never go back to its old dimensions."

— Oliver Wendell Holmes, Jr.

The first definition of dimensions is more traditional; the second will take you places you may not have gone before!

To understand the fundamental building blocks of reality, you need to understand dimensions, dimensionality, and what density of matter really is. Here's one quick breakdown of what some folks think are the first ten dimensions. M-theory in quantum physics argues that eleven dimensions potentially exist, and bio-sonic string theories suggest as many as twenty-six dimensions. I'm sure before this book goes to print, someone will have another theory of even more dimensions! We'll just stick to ten, which is enough to make the point.

First Dimension: Length.

Second Dimension: Height.

Third Dimension: Depth.

Fourth Dimension: Time.

Fifth Dimension: A world slightly different than ours.

Sixth Dimension: A plane of all possible worlds, all with the same start conditions (Big Bang).

Seventh Dimension: A plane of all possible worlds with different start conditions.

Eighth Dimension: A plane of all possible worlds, each with different start conditions, each branching out indefinitely.

Ninth Dimension: All possible worlds, starting with all possible start conditions, and the laws of physics are all completely different.

Tenth Dimension: Infinite Possibilities.

"We live in a universe composed of 100 percent original consciousness. As such, we are dreaming the dream of Creation, each one of us playing our individual part of experiencing the universe from our own unique viewpoint."

— Owen Waters

Another popular thought is that there are twelve dimensions. Nine are basic dimensions that function together in an intertwined harmony, and then there are three dimensions that consciousness brings to the nine dimensions. Put another way, the dimensions under this model are all facets of consciousness as it creates energy, space, and motion. Under this model, there are four categories of dimensions: Motion, Space, Energy, and Consciousness.

First Dimension: Physical time in motion.

Second Dimension: Feelings in motion (emotion).

Third Dimension: Thoughts in motion.

Fourth Dimension: Spherical Separation.

Fifth Dimension: Circular Separation.

Sixth Dimension: Linear Separation.

Seventh Dimension: Electric Energy (building block of physical matter).

Eighth Dimension: Magnetic Energy (primal field of the Universe).

Ninth Dimension: Life or Etheric Energy.

Tenth Dimension: Consciousness templates for the

Infinite Universe.

Eleventh Dimension: Female Creator Consciousness.

Twelfth Dimension: Male Creator Consciousness.

If we are fairly certain there are ten or twelve dimensions and both of those models include Infinite Possibilities, why go beyond that to a model of twenty-six dimensions, or even beyond that? What is there beyond Infinite Possibility? Am I right? Whew! Stop while we can still wrap our heads around this stuff!

So what does all this mean to you? It means that everything you see is something more than simply how it appears. Everything you think you know is something else. Every possibility, any possibility, infinite possibilities, exist. There is something much larger going on here; there is a knowingness and a predictability while at the same time a seeming chaos. Chaos is actually a result of free will. (We'll go into details on free will and chaos in Volume II.) Everything else is a result of the Great Parent, the mind of All That IS. You, me, *us*!

Every possibility exists—that's what makes sense to me. It *feels* right. I like the twelve-dimension model. This is where it gets really difficult to wrap your head around the idea, and it's okay if you don't want to, as long as you accept that the possibilities exist. For each choice you're given, you have the ability to make any choice you wish. Each wish gets lived out because it is a thought, and each thought is a thing—a thing, a frequency, or an energy. If this is a new concept to you, it may be overwhelming at first. Don't stress about it; it's not as frightening as it may seem. In fact, when you truly understand what's going on, you will realize there's never anything to be afraid of!

String theories seem to explain what's going on the best.

"Einstein was searching for String Theory. It not only reconciles General Relativity to Quantum Mechanics, but it reconciles Science and the Bible as well."

— Roy H. Williams

Briefly, as Roy H. Williams says: "String theory describes energy and matter as being composed of tiny, wriggling strands of energy that look like strings. And the pitch of a string's vibration determines the nature of its effect." It is the consciousness of the string that controls the pitch, or vibration (my interpretation).

But we don't need to go into this in depth. Other theories about dimensions stop at seven quite happily, saying that even at seven dimensions, we can know everything in an instant.

We are made out of invisible energy, not tangible matter. So go ahead, look around the room. Look at your hand, your kid, your spouse, or your pet, your car, your house, this book.... And realize it's all an illusion. Why do you suppose you are here, in your illusion, participating in this grand adventure?

Write any ideas you may have about why you are here now. Are there times when you have been aware of more than three dimensions? When did that happen and what were those other dimensions?

1)

2)

3)

4)

5)

"We are more often frightened than hurt; and we suffer more from imagination than reality."

— Lucius Anneals Seneca

COLORING YOUR SACRAL CHAKRA

"Sexual love is joyous; it is exuberant in its appreciation of love's mystery and life's gift."

— James Nelson

The color of your sacral chakra is deep orange. To balance your sacral chakra, you can wear deep orange-colored clothes, surround yourself with deep orange things, and eat dark orange foods.

If your sacral chakra is balanced, you'll be graceful in your movements, have healthy boundaries, and it will be easy for you to experience pleasure.

If your sacral chakra is out of balance, you may have a pleasure addiction or excessive emotions, be overly sensitive, or have low self-esteem.

You can use the following clearing statements to bring your sacral chakra into balance:

- ♥ "I release and let go of any and every thing that is stealing my self-esteem and preventing me from feeling whole and powerful."
- ♥ "I release and let go of any and every thing that is preventing me from letting go of my feelings of sexual discomfort."
- ♥ "I release and let go of any and every thing that is interfering with my ability to feel pleasure and preventing me from being able to experience the joys of life."

- ♥ "I release and let go of any and every thing that steals my joy."

"To give vent now and then to his feelings, whether of pleasure or discontent, is a great ease to a man's heart."

— Francesco Guicciardini

Chapter 3

LIVING IN NO-TIME

"When a man sits with a pretty girl for an hour, it seems like a minute. But let him sit on a hot stove for a minute—and it's longer than any hour. That's relativity."

— Albert Einstein

In Chapter 2 of this section, we discussed the wall of dimension and came to see the possibility of infinite outcome. The next challenging wall I want to walk you through is time, or the fourth dimension. Even though time was covered in the breakdown of dimensions, it requires some special attention in and of itself.

Back in the mid-1990s, I was living in Michigan and working in outside sales. I spent most of my time in my car, driving around the countryside to visit clients and potential customers, and I would listen to productivity and self-improvement tapes (yes, tapes) as a way to make good use of my time in the car. One day, I happened to be listening to a series by Deepak Chopra when I heard him say, "There is no such thing as time. Time is something we created in order to experience the physical world. Everything is really happening at once."

Talk about making one's head spin! In that moment, my world was rocked. Even though I didn't understand how it worked at all, it instantly made sense to me. It was a piece of the puzzle of life that I had been seeking without knowing what it was I was looking for, and in that moment, the puzzle piece slid into place. Life suddenly made more sense. I'd had some experiences in time travel and past life regression, which when considered in this new light, suddenly were much more understandable and even became magical. (It's always nice when the external world validates something in us that had previously been labeled crazy, even if only in our mind.)

"If time is not real, then the dividing line between this world and eternity, between suffering and bliss, between good and evil, is also an illusion."

— Herman Hesse

Zen Buddhism, in particular, stresses this very significant insight. Here's the Sixth Patriarch, Ch'an Master Hui-neng:

> In this moment there is nothing that comes to be. In this moment there is nothing that ceases to be. Thus there is no birth-and-death to be brought to an end. Thus the absolute peace in this present moment. Though it is at this moment, there is no limit to this moment, and herein lies eternal delight.

When you grasp the deep meaning of that statement, it should make everything you know in the core of your soul rush in—that you are one with all and that you are manifested in third-dimension physical form on Eden/Earth/Gaia. You are here to fulfill a purpose, and when you stay in the now, as that person, as you, there is such feeling of wonder and possibility it's hard to explain. (That's what this whole book is—my attempt to explain and help show you how to experience it yourself!)

"You will never find time for anything.
If you want time you must make it."

— Charles Buxton

If there's no such thing as time, and everything is happening at once, how does that work? What about history? What about past lives? We know people have experienced other lives, of living in other times. I myself am aware of a variety of different times that I've lived (or visited), and I remember little snippets of things that happened to me in those lives. I am also someone who is precognitive, meaning I see the future.

I don't understand it entirely, and what I do understand is not easy to explain, but I'll give it a try.

As St. Augustine said, "What then is time? If no one asks me, I know what it is. If I wish to explain it to him who asks, I do not know."

Later on, in Volume III, in the section on healing, I'll share some of my personal experiences to help illustrate what I'm about to explain here, and that provide some tangible proof for those of you skeptical of past life experiences. For some, it is easier for us to access what we would term "past lives" than it is for us to access our lives in the future, even though they should be equally accessible.

Imagine layers of clear glass, endless layers of clear glass, each of them being different lives. These different lives are all different versions of ourselves, living out different experiences. Remember the infinite possibilities from the dimensions chapter. See them layered in parallels, in a circle around you with you in the center. Picture the markings of a clock face. The arrow of time is normally facing the twelve. You're standing facing twelve, and as you stand there, you are in the *now*. "Time," which is memory, is accumulating around the circle.[13] The future also exists around the circle. At any moment, you can point the arrow to a different point on the circle. You can peer into any moment in time. For some reason, in my experience, it works more easily looking at your memories than it does your future, with things like past-life regressions. People don't understand the power of visualization as it pertains to the future. We actually create the future every day when we plan ahead for tomorrow. There are, however, people who see the future. Accuracy is more of an issue looking forward and because free will is always at play, the future is a variable (I'd say one of my most difficult talents is the ability to see all the different possibilities at once.)

When your focus shifts from the moment you are in, and you think about the past or the future, you're in essence traveling through time—either going backwards or forwards in your memory or imagination because nothing other than the moment ever exists.

---

13 Check the book website www.WalkingThroughYourWalls.com for videos illustrating this concept.

"The thing I like most about time is that it's not real. It's all in the head. Sure, it's a useful trick if you wanna meet someone at a specific place in the universe to have tea or coffee. But that's all it is, a trick. There's no such thing as the past, it exists only in the memory. There's no such thing as the future, it exists only in our imagination. If our watches were truly accurate the only thing they would ever say is now."

— Damien Echols

We, in whatever year we happen to be in, can look back on history to whatever place we wish to gaze upon, and really what we're looking at is a different moment of *now* because we ourselves are not going anywhere, except in our minds, with our consciousness.

"Eternity is not, and cannot, be found tomorrow—it is not found in five minutes—it is not found in two seconds. It is always already Now. The present is the only reality. There is no other."

— Ken Wilber

All the nows know about all the other nows; it only appears separate in this physical plane. In reality, we all know and are a part of all of history and can reference each other and other moments in time whenever we want, whenever we tune in.

Something to bear in mind is that because of the principle of oneness, all lives lived are your life. Every life that has ever been lived is your past life. Don't focus on that too hard right now; until you have the whole picture, that might feel a little creepy or overwhelming.

Let me introduce another angle that must be taken into consideration.

The lives you see as you move through the parallels are lives that vibrationally match your current life. You might be seeing a life you have lived yourself, or you might be seeing any other life that vibrationally matches where you are in the now. You have access to all lives, but to visit with one, you have to match its frequency. If you want to visit elsewhere, you need to shift your frequency.

That is how you can move through the parallels; you can move laterally at any time you wish, but only to lives and situations that vibrationally match the life you are in, or the vibrational frequency that you are emitting in the moment.

It is my impression that we are given these opportunities to see our problems from different angles. Once we heal ourselves on any parallel, we heal ourselves on all parallels. I believe that by clearing a multi-lifetime problem in any life, it clears in all lives, and all lives then reflect that healing. Therefore, as you raise your vibrational frequency in this lifetime, all lifetimes and all lives benefit. The whole benefits because we are all one and connected, and there is only now.

You have free will in your third-dimensional body. You came here to do something, to have some experience, to accomplish some objective. You have a purpose—to have a certain kind of relationship, to build a certain thing, to write a certain book, etc. Perhaps you are here to heal a broken family dynamic, or to learn patience or forgiveness, or perhaps to experience a life of poverty after having a life of decadence, or to live a life of comfort after living a life of poverty, etc. Perhaps you are here to help awaken others to why they are here.

Because of free will, each time you take a step, make a choice, or decide for whatever reason to deviate from the direction of your purpose, you lower your vibrational frequency and delay the inevitable, which is your growth. We never come here to be stagnant, and if we become stagnant, that is a misalignment of purpose, which may or may not be the result of an energetic feedback loop.

You don't have free will not to complete your mission or your spirit and soul's purpose, but you do have free will on when and how, so it can be in this lifetime or another. If you leave this plane and you haven't accomplished what you came here to do, you'll just have to come back again into the third-dimensional realm to accomplish it.

It's critical that you determine what you came here in this lifetime, in this dimension, to do, if you haven't already. The sooner you are able to determine your purpose, the sooner you can make the most of each now!

Some have said that we human beings are the only ones who can think into the future, but I've seen animals do it, so we're not the only ones. I knew a dog once that every day in the afternoon, would get up, walk a mile to a lake, go swimming, and then come home. It's documented that pets left home will start to get restless at the exact time their owners leave work to return home. One need only say to our dogs "Want to go to the beach?" to see them go absolutely wild. Each of these is an example of how animals are able to imagine an alternate reality. We are able to use our memories and imagination to create new situations in our heads, and through a process of reflection and projection, we envision the future. Animals, certainly dogs, can do the same thing. Who is to say everything can't?

According to Nassim Haramein, every thought, every move you make, is being recorded by what he calls "spacetime." As we saw in the last chapter, the reality we live in is made up of three dimensions. When we add time to the equation of reality, we discover it is the fourth dimension. All events, places, moments in history, actions, and so on, are described in terms of their location in space-time. Each atom or particle exists on its own world-line, which can be dissected to locate the particle in different locations in space and time.

In Chapter 6 of this section, we'll look at some real-life illustrations to help make this discussion of time easier to visualize. You and I could spend a lot of time going into the theory of the space-time continuum. Or we can just take what we need from the discussion, which is that time doesn't exist, and let it go at that.

The whole point here is that the discovery that there is no time and that all lives are one life—your life, my life, our lives together—should spur you to want to know the rest, to know it all, to know the point of it all, and how to make the most out of your life.

One of the hardest lessons you may ever learn is the lesson that it's not about the *why* of something! It's about the *what*! I say that because it was one of the hardest lessons for me to learn. My entire life I've been asking, "Why? Why? Why?" It doesn't matter why. In fact, you can get way too distracted worrying about why things have happened. It's about what you are going to do about it! Your reaction to anything is the only thing you have control over, so the whole point of life is to stay in the *now* and be mindful.

Can you think of some times in your life when time has seemed to collapse or you've seen into the distant past or the future?

1)

2)

3)

4)

5)

"Tell me, what is it you plan to do with your one wild and precious life?"

— Mary Oliver

FEELING YOUR SACRAL CHAKRA

"Do what makes you happy, be with who makes you smile, laugh as much as you breathe, and love as long as you live."

— Rachel Ann Nunes

Your sacral chakra governs your creativity and personal relationships in addition to the physical areas, such as your liver and upper intestines, reproductive organs, pancreas, and stomach. When your sacral chakra is blocked or out of balance, you may suffer some physical problems such as back pain, sexual or fertility problems, urinary problems, knee troubles, and a loss of appetite for life and its pleasures. You may feel worried or anxious.

Here are some clearing statements for your sacral chakra:

- ♥ "I release and let go of any and every thing that is keeping me from experiencing pleasure to its fullest."
- ♥ "I release and let go of any and every thing that is preventing me from experiencing the beauty and wonder the Universe has to offer."
- ♥ "I release and let go of any and every thing that prevents my emotions from flowing through me in a healthy manner."

Here are some affirmations for your sacral chakra:

- ♥ "I have healthy boundaries, and I love and enjoy my body."

- "I am open to experiencing the present moment through my senses."
- "I take good care of my physical body, and I nourish my body with healthy food and clean water."

"Never apologize for showing feeling.
When you do so, you apologize for the truth."

— Benjamin Disraeli

Chapter 4

GRAPPLING WITH GRAVITY

"Most gravity has no known origin.
Is it some exotic particle? Nobody knows."

— Neal deGrasse Tyson

In the previous chapter, we tackled the wall of time. I'm hopeful you're still with me! These walls are not easy to understand, much less walk through. If you are still with me, your perseverance will serve you well, and you will go far!

In this chapter, we're going to look closely at the force of gravity and the role it's playing in our lives. I fondly call it the Grief of Gravity. We'll need to take a quick look at all the basic forces of nature, but I believe we should be particularly interested in gravity, much more than we've ever been taught. I will explain why.

You may not realize it, but as you are sitting here reading this, you are being influenced by the forces of nature. Everything in the universe is made from a few basic building blocks called fundamental particles, governed by four fundamental forces. Our best understanding of how these particles, and three of the forces, are related to each other, is encapsulated in the Standard Model of Particle Physics.

Although you may be able to think of a number of different forces, when you strip appearances away, all forces are either electromagnetic or gravitational in nature. When you realize that gravity is actually the weakest of the two, it becomes even clearer that everything is really energy!

We then need to realize that there are both strong and weak energies in the area of electromagnetism and gravity.

This is how it has come to be said that there are four forces in nature:

1. Electromagnetism
2. Gravity
3. Strong
4. Weak

Each of these four have different strengths and ranges of influence.

1. Electromagnetism is much weaker than the strong force and much stronger than the gravitational force, with an infinite range. It can be attractive or repulsive, but it only acts between matter carrying an electrical charge. Its force causes electric and magnetic effects.

2. Gravitational force is the weakest, but with infinite range; it is always attractive and acts between any two (all) bits of matter in the universe. It is what is responsible for keeping the universe in order and everything in its place. Mass is its source.

3. The strong force is very strong, but very short ranged and operates at the subatomic level. It is responsible for holding the nuclei of atoms together. Normally attractive, it can be repulsive under certain circumstances.

4. The weak force is much stronger than gravity, but it operates at subatomic particle level and is responsible for radioactive decay and neutrino interactions. It has a very short range and is very weak.

"The split between religion and science is relatively new. Isaac Newton, who first worked out the laws by which gravity held the planets and even the stars in their traces, was sufficiently impressed by the scale and regularity of the universe to ascribe it all to God."

— Seth Shostak

Why do you care about these forces? You need to care because they are operating on you constantly. Up until now, I wouldn't be surprised if you never thought about them. Yet gravity, in particular, I believe is affecting you in ways you want to know about and learn to work with.

I only wish to touch on the highlights here, in order to get us where we need to be. Volume II will discuss the effects of gravity upon us in a bit greater detail.

Scientists like one solution, so disliking the four forces idea, they have been searching for years for a unified theory. Einstein spent the last years of his life pursuing this. It has not yet been found, but there have been some recent discoveries that might lead to its discovery. This field of science is constantly undergoing discovery. Stephen Hawkins has searched for "The Theory of Everything." It has not yet been found.

In the meantime, on July 4, 2012, two sets of scientists, working independently at the Large Hadron Collider at CERN (the European Organization for Nuclear Research), discovered "Higgs-Boson," which some are calling a fifth force of nature. What's interesting here is that although scientists have discovered the Higgs-Boson, as of publication, they don't yet understand it or know what it means.

Further complicating things, on December 15, 2015, two sets of scientists working independently at the same collider announced that they had seen traces of what could be a new fundamental particle of nature, perhaps a cousin to Higgs-Boson.

Let's see whether we can make some sense of all of this! Although gravity is one of the forces, gravity would appear to operate on its own, making a unified theory difficult for scientists. The "Standard Model" of the Universe excludes gravity and states that the other three fundamental forces of nature result from the exchange of force-carrier particles, which belong to a larger group called "bosons."

Particles of matter transfer discrete amounts of energy to other particles by exchanging bosons with each other. Each fundamental force has its own corresponding boson. The photon carries electromagnetic force. The gluon carries the strong force. The weak force is carried by the W and Z bosons.

Scientists have been looking for the "graviton" boson, which would carry the force of gravity, but as yet, they have not found it, although they may be close. This newer approach is looking at the force of gravity as particles and waves, but to date, there has been no proof or explanation of how gravity works. We know that on Earth what goes up must come down, and we know the planets will stay in orbit due to gravity. We just don't know how or why!

So, currently, the "Standard Model" that physicists use to describe the universe excludes the force of gravity because they can't figure out how to fit it in.

The General Theory of Relativity and Quantum Theory are difficult to fit into a single framework, and since there has been no mathematical compatibility discovered between the two, the discovery of a Unified Theory and, more recently, the predictions of supersymmetry remain elusive.

Gravity does seem to belong outside of the model because only matters of density—like the human body and anything in this physical plane, like the planets, etc.—are impacted by gravity. Given what we learned in Chapter 2 of this section, that we are made out of invisible energy, not tangible matter, it's a little hard to wrap our heads around what gravity is impacting. What is our physical body then if we are more energy than tangible matter?

It is the *form of matter* that gravity influences, like the sum of our trillions upon trillions of cells. Things at the micro level seem to operate independently of gravity, but groupings of cells gives them mass, which is what gravity has force over. The force of gravity appears to function in a beautiful symmetry that is replicated throughout the universe.

To understand a little better, it might help to realize that the force of gravity upon us gives us our weight. When you step on a scale, the scale reads how much gravity is acting on your body. The larger your body, the more gravity.

Einstein believed that gravity is a distortion of the space-time continuum and not a force at all, which would support it not being included in the Standard Model. There have been some recent developments in the area of gravity and Einstein's theory of relativity and the space-time continuum. Scientists think they have heard the sound of two black holes colliding. "We are all over the moon and back," said Gabriela González of Louisiana State University, a spokeswoman for the LIGO Scientific Collaboration—short for Laser Interferometer Gravitational-Wave Observatory. "Einstein would be very happy, I think."

What is imperative for you to understand is that electromagnetism and other microscopic forces of nature are hundreds of millions of trillions of trillions time stronger than gravity. Yet here we are, stuck on Planet Earth, not going anywhere. So, for a moment, just try to wrap your head around that. Gravity is what is keeping everything in order, but it's the *weakest force.*

We're made out of energy, which is a bazillion times stronger. Do you feel that strong? Do you feel that powerful? I bet you don't, but why?

Gravity! It's grave! Defined, gravity is the force that (on Earth) draws a body toward the center of earth. Well, that's a downer, isn't it?

Seriously, it's drawing everything on Earth downwards toward Earth, toward the core.

Now think about this: You are an energetic being, more space than solid, and every one of your trillions of trillions of cells are spinning and vibrating. How much harder do they have to work to spin when gravity is pulling them downward toward the center of the Earth? Here is where all of this exploration starts to get interesting.

Think back to Chapter 2 of this section, where we talked about energy and how that's what everything is. You've likely heard about auras and how everyone has one. If you're not familiar with them, you can google "human aura" and look at the images. You can also google the term "torus energy" or "toroidal energy" and check out those images. There's a great composite graphic that shows the torus energy field around a tree, an apple, a human, and Earth.[14]

Now imagine an aura around all of Earth/Gaia. See the bands of energy encompassing Earth and passing through the poles, through the core, enveloping the entire planet. That is the aura of Earth, if you will, but it's also something more. It's the connection to the energetic grid of the Universe, of the One Great Mind, of the Parent, of All That IS, to AAH.

We as humans (and all things really) have an energetic aura similar to the Earth's aura. At one time, we were directly connected to the Earth's aura. Some of us are still connected or have re-connected, but most of us are not connected. In fact, many of us don't realize there is a connection to make—that's how disconnected we are!

Think of yourself as a grape, hanging down to Earth from the energetic grid that surrounds Earth. Visualize your energetic aura all around you and the core passing through you going

---

14 Be sure to check the *Walking Through Your Walls* Website for some interesting images and videos about toroidal energy. WalkingThroughYourWalls.com

upwards and connecting to the energetic grid surrounding Earth. Each of us is connected through our core to that grid. That's how each of us starts out: connected to Source, to the Great Parent, to All That IS, to AAH.

Now, picture the effect of gravity on each of us grapes.... It's pulling us down, down, down, down to the center of the Earth. Think of a rubber band—what happens when you pull and pull and pull on it? In the very middle, it gets thinner and thinner and thinner. If it's pulled too hard, it snaps. This is what has happened to most of us—we've become disconnected from Source, from the Power That IS. Gravity has pulled us down and strained our connection, and in many cases, it's caused a complete disconnection. We're snapped off the branch of the All That IS, wandering around disconnected.

How did gravity form in the first place? I like to tell the story this way:

So we're in the midst of creation. As the Great One Mind, we are contemplating what we want to experience. Perhaps in the beginning there was just darkness and we wanted light, so we started by creating the suns and stars of the Universe. *AAH*, we thought, *now that's beautiful!* So we moved on into further creation. We moved through the dimensions and settled upon the third dimension as the perfect playground of creation.

But at some point, we ran into a problem. We wanted to put things on things, but things kept flying off. So we thought up gravity. It wasn't the first thing we tried, but it worked! There, that fixed things fine. Or so we thought. We never considered the ramifications on our energetic beings when we did it. I think we were just too excited, having too much fun.

When you take a detached view of creation, and you think about how it actually would have worked, it's just like anything else. The greatest architect can build something that is flawed because of some unseen thing, some unanticipated influence, some unpredicted consequence of design. Since all of creation is a result of the One Great Mind, of AAH, All is Always Well. There is nothing to regret or feel badly about. It is what it is. And it is Divine, it is perfect in its imperfection. Imperfection allows for growth.

There is another side effect of gravity. Sure, it has kept us on Earth, which is where The Great One Mind wants us, and it has kept Earth and the planets in orbit; in fact, it has kept order in the Universe. But it has also contributed to the separation consciousness that we suffer from; it has helped to create the problems of desperate fear and unhappiness that humanity faces.

The mass of humanity is walking around in what I, and others, refer to as "separation consciousness." Most people are completely unaware of their eternal life, of their incredible potential, of their amazing talents and unlimited future. Even I, aware of all of my potential from the very beginning, have had to work in a concentrated, intentional way to overcome the many influences of this physical third dimension. I am still working on them because I have yet to walk through a wall physically.

Fear is the unanticipated side effect of gravity. Yeshua Ben Joseph came to show us how to raise our vibrations—how to overcome our fears and have faith in our ability as given to us by AAH. He spoke to us about love—as have so many others.

But what grips us is fear. What rules our lives is fear. We are grave our whole lives, and then we go to our graves!

This is what I believe happened to Adam in the Garden—Adam's electromagnetic connection to the Great Parent, his energetic flow, became strained by the effects of gravity. The Voice of AAH became dimmer or harder to hear, making the snake's voice more powerful and easier to hear. Instead of knowing himself what right action was, he couldn't hear the voice inside, he couldn't hear his Spirit, and he couldn't feel his connection to his Source. Adam, instead, turned to external sources for answers and the truth.

Because electromagnetism is the strongest force in the Universe, and we are energetic beings, light beings, it seems to me that the way we reconnect with our power, the power of the Universe, and with Source, with the Great One Mind, our Parent, to AAH, is to raise our vibration. We have to counter the effects of gravity in order to reconnect. As we raise our vibration, we will be attracted to similar frequency, and similar frequency will be attracted to us. As we raise our frequency, we also become more, and more, light beings. At some point, in a light being state, walking through walls, walking on water, becomes completely possible.

Gravity is challenging us in every moment in these endeavors! This is the talent that Yeshua Ben Joseph had. He had the ability to raise his frequency to such an extent that he became weightless and could walk, seemingly, on water. In theory, walking through a wall in this state should be equally possible. Yeshua embodied his light body. His light body was weightless because as light, gravity had nothing upon which to give mass to. Without mass, gravity is irrelevant.

Remember, gravity is the weaker of the two forces, but with infinite range. But the strongest force is electromagnetism, so you do not have to work hard to reconnect with Source. It is not difficult—it simply takes intention, mindfulness, and attention. Think of magnets. Each of us has a magnet on the top of our head that is connected to the magnet of Universal Power, the Great One, the All That IS, to AAH.

Astronaut Scott Kelly is living proof of the force of gravity. After living a year in space, he returned in February 2016 two inches taller than when he left. His tallness was short-lived, however, shrinking back to his normal height almost within hours of his return.

Do you ever feel like gravity is pulling you down? Do you think it's possible to feel lighter than you do? Are you familiar with feeling disconnected? What other thoughts do you have about gravity?

1)

2)

3)

4)

5)

"Because there is a law such as gravity, the universe can and will create itself from nothing."

— Stephen Hawking

HEALING YOUR SACRAL CHAKRA

"Emotion always has its roots in the unconscious and manifests itself in the body."

— Irene Claremont de Castillejo

Your sacral chakra is your emotional energy center, and it is in charge of your sense of self-gratification. Your sacral chakra is also the seat of guilt when wounded. What is guilt? Guilt is the feeling you've done something wrong—except it's not just regret or remorse; it's much, much worse because it's laden with emotional baggage. Guilt is not a genuine emotion, but rather a learned or conditioned response. Guilt is really more about other people than it is about you. We learn guilt because people teach it to us.

For some reason, this truth about guilt is a lesson I was born knowing. When people tried to guilt me into feeling badly about something, it never worked because I would always think to myself, "At any given moment, I'm always trying to do my best; if I'm always trying to do my best, what do I have to feel guilty about?"

Lucky for me, or I might not be here writing this book. If I'd taken on all that others wanted me to feel guilty about, I'd likely still be working on myself at a deep level—if I were still here at all.

I encourage you to consider where guilt fits into your life. Abandon guilt as soon as possible if you suffer from it. Remember, when others speak, the words they say are a reflection of them, not you. Do not take on others' projections. Be yourself; honor yourself.

You are a divine and special being. You have great value and capability, regardless of what others say they see in you. Even you don't likely understand your potential at this point because you don't realize the magnificent creature you really are yet.

To heal your sacral chakra, start with movement. Take up yoga, or dancing, or some other kind of movement therapy. Something that is not stressful, but allows you to explore your body and its capability.

"Movement is a medicine for creating change in a person's physical, emotional, and mental states."

— Carol Welch

You may find that you spend excessive time in a fantasy world, particularly a sexual fantasy world, rather than having actual relations with another human. When your sacral chakra is balanced, you'll be able to have comfortable contact with others, and you will feel at ease with your sexuality and with your body.

"It is said that each time we embrace someone warmly, we gain an extra day of life."

— Paulo Coelho

An afflicted sacral chakra can result in overindulgences of drugs or alcohol; a balanced sacral chakra allows you to enjoy the moment through the practice of mindfulness.

Meditating is another way to help balance your sacral chakra.

Here are some affirmations to help clear your sacral chakra:

- "I am radiant, beautiful, and strong and enjoy a healthy and passionate life."
- "I honor my body as a sacred vessel and treat it with respect."
- "I am grateful for the joy of being me and for each moment of life."
- "I go with the flow with grace and ease; I allow life to live itself."
- "I receive pleasure and abundance with every breath I take."

"Movement never lies. It is a barometer telling the state of the soul's weather."

— Martha Graham

Chapter 5

PIERCING THE ILLUSION OF REALITY

"Reality is merely an illusion, albeit a very persistent one."

— Albert Einstein

As I mentioned earlier, it was a bit difficult to figure out the order of these walls. We've covered the wall of dimensions, the wall of time, and the wall of gravity.

The wall of reality is perhaps the tallest and thickest and the hardest one to overcome or walk through because it's so pervasive. It encompasses everything physical and is such a persistent illusion that it will take great effort to overcome.

The "law of the conservation of energy" states that energy can neither be created nor destroyed. The saying, "It's all energy" has become quite common, and when we say that phrase, people will nod their heads in agreement and seem to know what it means. It is my experience, as I am certain it is yours, that people are *not* moving through their lives with this knowingness in the forefront of their minds. Mostly, I suspect, because no one is explaining how to do that.

"If you want to find the secrets of the universe, think in terms of energy, frequency, and vibration."

— Nikola Tesla

Let's take a quick moment to review. And let me note that from here on out, because we have already established that the "truth" is to be had readily, I am not going to slow things down further with excessive details and factual citations. I ask you to trust me. I will not say anything that is not my explicit experience, firsthand knowledge, or at least the result of some research. I make nothing up. I have the highest of integrity and intend to provide you with only viable information, but if I take the time to back up everything I am going to say in the coming pages, this book will become a tome. (It already has, hence the three volumes. Let's keep it to three!)

When we discuss energy and the energetic field, and oneness, what people seem to be missing is the actual scientific proof. And the proof that I use is the simplest proof there is: If we put anything, absolutely anything, under the strongest microscope we have, it looks the same. It doesn't matter what it is you look at, it looks the same. It looks the same because it is the same!

"Our species needs, and deserves, a citizenry with minds wide awake and a basic understanding of how the world works."

— Carl Sagan

Everything is an illusion and it takes real, hard thought and focus to understand that absolutely everything we see, touch, and feel is an illusion. There is nothing solid. That which is solid is an illusion because, as we know, everything is more space than solid, and everything is moving, spinning, and vibrating.

"Everything is energy and that's all there is to it. Match the frequency of the reality you want and you cannot help but get that reality. It can be no other way. This is not philosophy. This is physics."

— Albert Einstein

What this means, then, is that it is 100 percent critical we be *conscious* as we move though the field of energy that is life because the field of consciousness is everything and everywhere! It becomes imperative, per Einstein, that we understand our frequency and control it.

Science has proven that there is nothing solid.

"A man cannot step in the same river twice."

— Heraclitus

Everything we see is more space than matter. We see things because they are vibrating at different frequencies, which gives an illusion of matter. We see color because the different frequencies absorb and reflect light at different ranges on a color wheel. In reality, as Einstein says, everything we see is an illusion. Nothing is real in a tangible way.

Here's the problem. Most people hear this, nod their heads, and say, "Yeah, okay." And they go right on doing things as they have always done them.

When I first heard this, it rocked my world, and it continues to rock my world on a daily basis because I understand that the only thing that can possibly make any sense about how my chair or the bed I sleep on will hold me up is that the particles that make up these things have agreed to participate in the illusion!

It's the only thing that makes sense to me. There really is no other explanation.

Although there is more space than matter in any given particle, the space itself is also filled with energy. So not only is nothing solid, but everything is energy, including space—everything is energy and motion. All of life is made up of about 100 elements. Elements are things that cannot be broken down into smaller components. Every element is made up of atoms, and each atom has electrons, and the electrons are always moving. Therefore, at some level, everything around you is moving.

"Get over it, and accept the inarguable conclusion. The universe is immaterial—mental and spiritual."

— Richard Conn Henry

So what does it mean that everything is made up of these atoms of mostly space and all energy, constantly spinning with their own unique energy signature, yet all of a similar appearance?

This study of energy is quite broad, and we could spend months just delving into this topic. Let's do as Richard Conn Henry suggests and accept the inarguable conclusion.

Let me share a story with you that illustrates this inarguable conclusion that everything is immaterial. A few years ago, I went to Connecticut to help a college friend's daughter who was returning her military family to the States and settling there. I took a knitting project with me—a really cool green and purple variegated chenille hoodie scarf. Oh, how I loved that scarf. I was really excited to finish it and wear it since it was going to be cold in February. I did finish the scarf before the family arrived, and I wore it a few times when we went out to eat or shopping.

On the last morning, I got all ready to take a shuttle to the bus I was taking to New Jersey to meet up with one of my best friends from high school. I was wearing the scarf as we waited for the shuttle. The whole family saw me wearing it. I got into the shuttle, a Town Car, wearing it. When we arrived at my destination (I was the only passenger), as the driver unloaded my luggage from the trunk, I reached to pull my scarf hood up, but the scarf was gone! I thought it had fallen off in the backseat, but it wasn't there. It wasn't anywhere to be found. To this day, that scarf is missing in action.

I'm sure you're thinking it fell off somewhere, but it didn't. I called my friend, who was certain she saw me wearing it when I got into the vehicle. She looked around the hotel lobby and checked with the front desk, just to be sure. No scarf.

I was totally blown away and mystified—until my friend in New Jersey and I went to visit a woman I knew on Long Island later that afternoon. When we got there, my friend Francine was excited to give me a scarf she had knitted for me. Suddenly, the missing scarf made sense. It may have crushed Francine, or at a minimum, it would have diminished her gift, if I had come walking in wearing my brand new scarf. Without a scarf, I was in need of one, which she could clearly see, making her gift all the more appropriate, needed, and appreciated!

I was glad to sacrifice the scarf I had made and loved to have that moment in which to say, "I just lost my scarf!" It was a beautiful experience, and I was grateful the Universe, My Great Parent, or Source, had intervened. I don't care by what name you want to call it. I've always been connected to it, so to me, there is no need for a name. We are connected to All That IS, and life is supposed to be happy, to be joyous—we're supposed to be having fun! This was a perfect example of a much larger picture and the universe conspiring miles away, fully knowing I was headed to see Francine!

Life is really just like a game: The Game of Life. We exist in a physical form in order to experience the wonders of life. We are the One Great Mind in expression. The wonderful things are the things we are here to experience. We come here to give of ourselves to others, to allow the One Great Mind the experience of connection and life in expression. We get to pick and choose many things, but we never pick misery. We never choose unhappiness. Misery and unhappiness are things humankind has created through its disconnection and subsequent misunderstanding of what is real.

"Every one of us is an aperture through which the whole cosmos looks out.... What you are basically deep deep down... far far in, is simply the fabric and structure of existence itself, and when you find that out, you laugh yourself silly."

— Alan Watts

So how did we get to be so unhappy? How did we become so miserable, sad, depressed, angry, fearful, shy, withdrawn, sick, sorry, destitute, poor, righteous, judgmental, mean, brutal, prejudiced, opinionated, rude, nasty, vindictive, manipulative, selfish, disgusted, delusional…and on and on it goes? How?

We have become disconnected from our energy centers, from ourselves. That's how.

You are an energetic being, and as an energetic being, you are connected to everything around you—you are connected to All That IS; you are connected to the One Great Mind; you are original source in expression. The unlimited energy of All That IS is constantly flowing through you, around you, to you, and away from you.

I am sure some of you know exactly what I am speaking of. Have you ever had the experience of walking into a room and suddenly feeling terrible? Or you left the house feeling fine, but by the time you got to the office, you felt you were tied in a knot? Understanding and tuning into the energy, your energy, and the energy around you, is a critical component to understanding life—and living harmoniously. We are basically hypnotized by appearances of matter, of the physical third dimension. We are hypnotized by the lives of others, and we think that they have something to do with us. We have been brainwashed by a history that has disempowered us, and we are constantly, instantly judging the world around us.

This judging based on appearances brings us many problems: we misunderstand things, we jump to conclusions, we make assumptions. We erroneously base our actions on these things, and often it brings us bitter disappointment. The problem is that even though we know things are not as they appear, we continue in our old ways.

As Fred Alan Wolf, Ph.D. and quantum physicist says: "Everything you know about the universe and its laws is more likely to be 99.99 percent wrong."

Together, we'll pierce the illusions once and for all! You will find your joy, your purpose, your perfect world.... Whatever you seek!

Can you think of five things you thought were one way but later discovered were not as you thought at all?

1)

2)

3)

4)

5)

"We're born alone, we live alone, we die alone. Only through our love and friendship can we create the illusion for the moment that we're not alone."

— Orson Welles

SINGING TO YOUR SACRAL CHAKRA

"The truest expression of a people is in its dance and in its music. Bodies never lie."

— Agnes de Mille

D is the musical note of the sacral chakra. Chanting and singing the tone of D will help you clear and balance your sacral chakra. Try dancing around while singing these statements in D:

- "I am full of vitality and joy."
- "I am comfortable in my body and with my sexuality."
- "I am comfortable with change and am easily adaptable."

"Socrates learned to dance when he was seventy because he felt that an essential part of himself had been neglected."

— Author Unknown

Chapter 6

REALIZING EVERYTHING IS CONSCIOUS

"There is a thinking stuff of which all things are made, and which in its original state permeates, penetrates, and fills the interspaces of the Universe."

— *Wallace D. Wattles*

In the past few chapters, we've just about deconstructed everything there is to deconstruct about reality. Now, let's really take a closer look at what it means for everything to be *thinking stuff*. Not only is everything more space than matter and moving, but it also is conscious, thinking matter. The One Great Mind is participating in every single second and every single thing in this grand illusion of the third dimension! Consciously, by choice, participating, creating, and living through all of us and through all things.

The Higgs-Boson, the fifth force that scientists have discovered, was predicted, and now that scientists have found it, they're not really sure what to do with it. I like to joke, "It's because they're scientists! They're staring at Oneness, at the Consciousness of All That IS, and they don't know it!"

I'm not sure who the first philosopher or scientist was who realized there is a consciousness in everything. I first grasped the idea when I read Wallace D. Wattles' work. Understanding that everything has a consciousness is a difficult and thick wall to get through.

To think: Whatever you're sitting on is conscious. Everything you touch is conscious. The walls of your house, the computer in your office, the clothes in your closet. *Everything*! Not just nature-made things, but man-made things also because everything is ultimately made of the same thing, and that same thing is all conscious. It is the mind of AAH—it is the One Great Mind, the All That IS. It's mind-boggling.

"Karma, when properly understood, is just the mechanics through which consciousness manifests."

— Deepak Chopra

What this all really means is that you should be including everything in your consciousness, in your awareness, in your orb and realm.

I like to say, "Everything is listening." This was an epiphany I had in 2013, after an episode where my mini-van actually communicated with me when it had something wrong with it, and the dealer was trying to send me home (135 miles away) with a problem—a huge problem, that with the "right" technician would end up being completely covered by recalls, after the "wrong" technician had given it a clean bill of health. The van acted crazy, really crazy, to give me a clue, and long story short, not only was there a lot wrong, the second technician knew about the recalls, which fixed everything at no cost to me. The entire suspension system, shocks, and struts. Given we live on a gravel road and had about 50,000 miles on the van, this was an extra special blessing! I was very grateful to my van for making sure it got fixed.

I try to talk to everything now. I thank everything around me for participating in my life. When I'm driving past beautiful scenery, I thank it as I pass. I apologize to the stapler when I drop it on the floor. When anything drops or falls over or is jarred in any way, I give compassion to it. Before I bang the pickle jar on the counter to loosen the lid, I apologize to it and ask permission. I know that the pickle jar doesn't mind because it is participating in this dimension, and banging a jar on the counter to open it is the way it's supposed to work. I daresay the jar and pickles would prefer the more gentle slap against an open palm, which also works.

Do you know why banging the jar works, by the way? The way I visualize it is this: All the molecules in the lid and jar are hanging on to each other—when you bang the lid on the counter, it shocks all of the molecules so they let go of each other for a moment. Some of them might be spinning faster for a few moments. This movement interferes with the force of gravity because the mass momentarily changes when everything lets go. When you try the lid again, it usually opens easily, and if not, a second bang usually takes care of it because everything was already stirred up. The second bang just further stirs things up.

But it's life that's working here! If you run the jar under hot water, a similar thing happens. As the molecules warm up, they start vibrating at a higher frequency. This can cause them to let go of each other because they're rushing around, which is what the heat does to them. This more mobile state will also allow you to loosen the lid.

It's alive! Everything is alive! You'll hear the term "sentient beings," but what most people don't realize is *everything* is a sentient being! Because everything is a part of the mind of all. Even the inanimate, even the manmade! Everything!

Life truly is like that childhood joke! "You know why you never tell a secret in the garden? Because the potatoes have eyes, the corn has ears, and the beans talk."

While the joke is intended to dissuade gossiping, what I mean here is that everything is influenced by your presence—by your energy, by your thoughts, by your spoken words. You being the observer in any moment changes the outcome of the moment, simply by your observation. If you interact with your world in a loving way, then your surroundings will reflect that. If you go through life angry and yelling, in resistance to what life is offering you, your environment and life experience will reflect that.

To get the most out of your experience in life is to realize that you are imprinting everything you come into contact with, with your energy and your thoughts. How do you want to imprint life? With love? With fear? With hate? With superiority? With bliss? With compassion? With greed? With meanness? With gratitude? With style? With derision?

Realize as you move through your day that you are attracting whatever you put out, and that everything around you is always paying attention because you are always in third-dimensional form, and absolutely everything is permeated with consciousness and involved, actively involved, even when in appearance everything is static.

> *"All matter originates and exists only by virtue of a force.... We must assume behind this force the existence of a conscious and intelligent Mind. This Mind is the matrix of all matter."*
>
> *— Max Planck*

I remember when I first realized that everything is paying attention, and that my energy, the frequency I am emitting, is impacting everything around me, and that as a result, everything is responding to me, and that frequency, whatever it may be. It was a bit intimidating and exhausting. It's nice to be able to hide. But there is ultimately no hiding in life. This is perhaps the hardest lesson: We must accept that we are 100 percent connected to everything around us. To connect fully with life at the level available to you, you must be open to the realization that everything is always listening, and responding, albeit in subtle ways, but responding nonetheless. It demands so much from you. At first, it will seem like a lot of work, trying to remember, trying to stay present and conscious of the mysterious way things are happening. You may be tempted to give up.

If you do "evil" (anything that does not serve the greater good of the whole might be termed as some form of evil), everything (and at a certain level, everyone) knows—you will be emitting that energy. The universe knows. The Great Parent knows. And All That IS knows because we are all *one*. The way energy works, you are magnetizing to you whatever you are emitting. If you are loving, grateful, accepting, everything knows—you will be emitting that energy and magnetizing that energy back to yourself. There is a matrix, if you will, from which there is no escape. Energy flows on this matrix; those who are open to love, receive more love; those who live in fear, experience more fearful lives because by putting their attention upon the fear, they are magnetizing fear to themselves. Energy flows where your attention goes.

Everything in nature, by the essence of what life is, wants nothing more than for you to be all that you want to be that's good. This is because the One Great Mind, the All That IS, AAH is in all.

Have you ever thought to yourself that inanimate objects might have minds of their own? Have you ever thought about why some people always seem to lose or break things? What other thoughts do you have about this chapter?

1)

2)

3)

4)

5)

"There is no god except the consciousness that exists in every molecule."

— Barbara Fields

BALANCING YOUR SACRAL CHAKRA

"Not only do we have a right to be happy, we have an obligation to be happy because our happiness has an effect on everyone around us."

— Dennis Prage

When your sacral chakra is balanced, you will be a warm and friendly person who radiates sincere interest without coming on too strong. You will be open to the world around you.

We tend to store emotional tension in our hips, so one way to help bring your sacral chakra into balance is to do some hip-opening exercises. There are many hip-opening positions in yoga.

As mentioned, movement and dance are great ways to bring balance to your sacral chakra, so lock the doors, pull down the shades, and dance like no one is watching!

This affirmation will help bring balance: "I live life passionately, with good health and vitality. I am unafraid to be myself. I am confident and am achieving my dreams!"

Chanting the word "BA" to the tone of D will help bring balance to this chakra.

"The tragedy is when you've got sex in the head instead of down where it belongs."

— D.H. Lawrence

Chapter 7

ACCEPTING NOTHING IS EVIL AND THERE'S NOTHING TO FEAR

"There is nothing that makes us feel so good as the idea that someone else is an evil-doer."

— Robert Staughton Lynd

In the last chapter, I asked you to realize that everything is conscious. That's asking a lot, I know, and now I'm going to ask you to believe that there is no evil in the world. There will be many who will argue with this chapter. The other walls are more neutral in their manifestation—no one is likely to argue hard with me about the principles I recapped about time, for example. Time is so speculative. Many people, however, are likely to want to argue over what I say about the existence of evil, or rather, the lack thereof.

I keep thinking I've covered the most difficult wall only to keep writing on to another also most difficult. Perhaps this is why we have never had a Handbook for Humanity before now; it's too darned hard to write! Some have called me a fool for trying.

Look, this is how I see it: I came here, I looked around, I tried to figure this place out, and I discovered there's no manual. Learning life seems so disorganized! It seems ridiculous to me that there is no manual, and that each of us is just supposed to "figure it out" ourselves from the mishmash we see around us. Get real. Everyone is looking around to each other for answers, and lots of people claim to have the answers, so we follow those paths, but we never seem to find the answers. Or we get some answers, but our problems don't go away.

In fact, the real answer is right in front of us, hidden in plain sight. It is within. It is in *you*. Your answer is in you. It is in *me*. My answer is in me. It is in *we*. When we go within, and we connect to our Shared Parent, the All That IS, we are one.

But few know that.

To me, this is just too important. I think we all need a manual. I know my grandchildren need a manual.

Alas, I have digressed! Back to *evil*! I'm dragging my feet! I can feel your resistance. I am challenging your belief system....

"What are you, crazy?" you ask. "There's no evil? Seriously?"

Yes, seriously, and let me explain to you why and how.

There is only One Great Mind, one All That IS, that is our Shared Parent, and there is only one substance, of which everything is made. This is where so many people take a wrong turn—they forget these things, or they never understood them to start with.

This is, in fact, the truth—many will try to keep this from you because once you truly understand it, to the degree this handbook will reveal, you are empowered with the power of creation. You are unlimited in your capability. This frightens people because they think they won't be able to control themselves, or that the power will corrupt them.

It is true that some humans will manifest the appearance of evil in this third-dimensional realm. Why they may do this is not for you to understand or worry about. The only thing you need to tend to is what are *you* going to do? As long as you keep your heart centered on your Spirit's purpose and remember that everything you do is for the good of the whole, you have nothing to worry about. You cannot misuse or abuse your power.

> *"Nothing in the nature around us is evil. This needs to be repeated since one of the human ways of talking oneself into inhuman acts is to cite the supposed cruelty of nature."*
>
> — *John Berger*

It's all a manifestation of the Great One Mind, the All That IS; it's all a manifestation of AAH, which means in essence, everything is heavenly, or divine, or celestial. This is a very difficult concept for most people. You want to cling to your fear because, in a twisted way, your fear makes you feel safe. You understand it—you feel comforted by it. When I suggest you let go of fear, many of you will feel fearful of that! Many of you will resist. Most of you.

It will likely take you some time to assimilate the information in this section, but hang in there and keep going. Working your way through this volume is the beginning of you getting your power back.

What more can I tell you about the lack of evil and there being nothing to fear? It rests with me to make the point so that you understand. It rests with me to take you to the point where you see that there is nothing other than the creation of the One Great Mind and that you are that mind.

Your I AM Presence is always available to you. Once you are connected to your I AM Presence, you will have a peace and harmony about you because you are connected to yourself and to the Great Parent. When you are connected to the Great Parent, to Your I AM Presence, you are in what is called by some Unified Consciousness and by others Non-Dual Consciousness. Unified Consciousness is the Collective Mind, which is the One Great Mind, the All That IS. Everything you see is a result of the One Great Mind. Therefore, everything is Celestial. Everything IS AAH. Similarly, yet in an alternate way, Non-Dual Consciousness is an open-ended state of compassion that pervades one's entire field of experience. Also an expression of AAH.

We are ALL One. We are all capable of what Yeshua Ben Joseph was capable of. We can *all* walk on water and do even greater things. However, until we all are walking on water (and even after), it is certain we all still have inner work to do. One of the most important pieces of inner work you will ever do is to learn how to see beyond the appearance of evil to the truth that everything you see is an illusion. You will see we are all one, here on a great expedition—we are here to have fun, to experience life, to learn lessons, to test ideas, to share, to love, to grow, to help one another, to serve each other. We are here to allow the One Great Mind, the All That IS, the AAH, to experience life in physical form.

"I believe the root of all evil is abuse of power."

— Patricia Cornwell

Since all is one, it is a given that our choices must always be for the good of the whole because if we choose what is best for ourselves, then the whole benefits. It is only when we see ourselves as separate, when we try to gain more than others through competitive means, when we are selfish, etc., that the appearance of evil appears. It remains an appearance because even in the choices of selfishness is the divine expression of a part of the whole, the All That IS.

Our planet is in the throes of terrorist attacks currently. "How," you ask, "can these acts be a part of AAH or anything but evil?" Think of these people and the acts they perpetrate this way: They are your training ground for learning the lesson of Infinite Love. "What about the people they kill?" you ask. Realize that it is *all* the Great One Mind's doing! It is a drama being acted out; it's not for you to know the entire script! Worry about your own role, your own script. These things that are happening likely do not affect you at all, except that you drag your attention to them. Until you can love everything and everyone, and until you see that life is a proving ground, a training ground for living the best you whom you can be, you will struggle.

Just before this book went to press, there was a big kerfuffle in the news over the death of the gorilla Harambe. Within minutes of his death, there were two petitions being passed around on social media. One to persecute the mother of the boy who caused the incident and the other against the zoo for shooting the animal. I ask you, what business is that of anyone's other than the people involved? It isn't, yet we cause ourselves daily misery being upset about all kinds of things, don't we?

Now that we have walked through all the earlier walls of reality, time, space, etc. I am hopeful you will be able to begin to see how what I suggest is possible. When you hear about someone you label evil, what is happening? You are judging. Fundamentally, it's really a thin wall—evil. It just seems thick because of your resistance. Your ego is judging things as evil, and your ego thinks it's in charge of your safety. So, in order to rid yourself of your belief in evil, you will have to teach your ego something new.

It is difficult to remember that the source of everything you are looking at is thought, and that it's all truly an illusion, a hallucination in your mind: creating a reality, where in fact there is no reality. Given this, can you understand that nothing created in this third-dimensional realm can be considered evil because it is all the result of thought—the thought of our Shared Parent, the Great One Mind, the All That IS?

There is only the appearance of evil. The question is not why is there evil, but what will be your response when the appearance of evil is brought to your attention? How will you react?

Taking this to the next level: There is also, for all the same reasons, nothing to be afraid of. Fear is nothing more than a lack of love. Everything is always exactly as it should be. There is a larger picture here to what is going on. We can't see the forest because of the trees.

"My life is perfect, even when it is not."

— Ellen DeGeneres

Everything is always perfect;[15] there are lessons being offered continually, constantly, infinitely. The lessons are about opening up your heart, about allowing love to flow. Gravity weighs us down and love appears elusive. Evil seems to prevail and be all around. Fear constricts us and we become shallow breathing, fearful creatures, sure of evil lurking around every corner. Once you learn how to walk through life fearless, you have found your power.

What are you afraid of? What or whom do you believe is evil?

1)

2)

3)

4)

---

15 For those of you who have suffered at the hands of abusers or endured any number of possible tortures, I do not mean to minimize your experience in any way! What I am suggesting is when you truly understand what is happening, you will be able to process the experiences with the understanding of their purpose and you will be able to let go of the feelings and emotions about what happened that cause you pain and unhappiness.

5)

"There is nothing evil save that which prevents the mind and shackles the conscience."

— Saint Ambrose

STRENGTHENING YOUR SACRAL CHAKRA

"Often the hands will solve a mystery that the intellect has struggled with in vain."

— Carl G. Jung

The element of the sacral chakra is water. When you have a healthy sacral chakra, you will be joyful with a healthy desire for what you want in life, and you will have an ability to ask freely and receive. It will be easy for you to be vulnerable while still feeling safe and secure. You are life. You'll have a healthy libido, and sex will be pleasurable without any guilt or shame or embarrassed feelings. With a balanced sacral chakra, you will be confident and have good self-esteem. You will not feel the need to seek others' approval, but rather, you are secure, joyful, and capable of both caring for yourself and assisting others.

The core wound of the sacral chakra is guilt. When you are clear and strong in your sacral chakra, you will not be subject to guilt. You will feel unafraid to live your truth and vitality. You know that you are life, that you have a reason to have your life. You are ready to live your purpose without concern for what others think and say, but rather, you answer to your internal guidance and truth system.

Here are some affirmations for strengthening your sacral chakra:

- "I enjoy life fully."
- "I reclaim my personal power to look after myself."
- "I live life passionately, with good health and vitality. I am unafraid to be myself. I am confident, and I am achieving my dreams!"

"The talent for being happy is appreciating and liking what you have, instead of what you don't have."

— Woody Allen

Chapter 8

LEARNING THE LIMITATION OF LANGUAGE

"I think perhaps the most important problem is that we are trying to understand the fundamental workings of the universe via a language devised for telling one another when the best fruit is."

— Terry Pratchett

This section, The Walls of Life, wouldn't be complete if we didn't talk a little bit about language, the power it has, and the role it plays in our lives.

Language is the method by which, in modern society, we share our ideas with each other, we share our intentions, and we share ourselves with each other, our thoughts, dreams, and secrets. Language is also one of the easiest platforms upon which we judge one another.

We judge others by the dialects they speak, by their accents, and often by a single word they may use. Howard Dean's "roar" during his run for the White House in 2004 killed his presidential campaign. A single word, roared to the crowd. At the end of a campaign rally, during just the last few minutes, Howard Dean allowed his excitement to take over, and after building up with a list of states he proposed to win, he issued a single "roar" to finish things off. And that was literally the end of Howard Dean. Although he is still active in politics, he stays behind the scenes for the most part.

The result of that roar is a stunning example of the limitations of language! You can search for it on YouTube and watch for yourself. It doesn't seem all that horrible, especially not in light of things that have transpired since. But the flow of energy was such that being President of the United States was not to be for Howard Dean.

This is a fitting illustration of the language's limitations and how we judge one another through our use of language.

It's amazing to observe how some people will think someone is wonderful while others think the same person is crazy or horrible.

Perhaps this is why emojis and memes have become so popular—to a certain extent, they transcend language.

"If you talk to a man in a language he understands, that goes to his head. If you talk to him in his own language, that goes to his heart."

— Nelson Mandela

In 2015, the Oxford Dictionary picked an emoji as its "Word of the Year," a decision that seemed to bring us full circle back to caveman days! However, pictures are much clearer than words. I think this is the essence of what the Nelson Mandela quote means. A graphic allows an observer to give it his or her own meaning, so you speak to the observer's heart rather than head with a graphic.

Some might dispute that it's obvious what an emoticon means. For example, an emoticon showing a big smile and tears might mean "tears of joy." I, however, have never used it because I was not sure what it meant!

I wonder whether people really do know that it means "tears of joy." The world does not seem like a joyful place when you look around; even if I had known what that emoji means, I wouldn't have used it very often..... And yet, Oxford English Dictionary declared the pictograph "tears of joy" its Word of the Year for 2015 based on its high usage." [16]

While pictures may be better at covering a feeling or message, and as the saying goes, "a picture is worth 1,000 words," spoken language is certainly a slippery slope. At a recent workshop, Jim W. Connolly, author of *iLead*, gave a wonderful example of just how slippery a slope language can be. Jim offered the illustration of his wife and himself planning for an emergency. He instructed his wife to go pack the things that were most important.

In emergency mode himself, Jim headed into the office to gather up the papers and other necessary things they would need.

---

16 http://blog.oxforddictionaries.com/2015/11/word-of-the-year-2015-emoji/.

When Jim returned to the bedroom to see how his wife was coming along with those emergency items, he found a strange selection of things set out on the bed: her wedding dress, some expensive boots, and as I recall, some furs.

"What's all this?" Jim asked. She explained that he had said to "Gather things that are important," and these were all things that were important to her.

Jim then clarified what he meant by "emergency," and instantly, she was off, gathering a completely different set of items.

"'Meow' means 'woof' in cat."

— George Carlin

Jim's story is a great example of how you can say something and believe you are being clear, but what you don't realize is that each person hears everything through his or her own filter. Each of us is a universe unto ourselves; everything is being filtered through each person's individual brain, personality, tendencies, past experiences, and beliefs.

How many arguments can you remember where you've said, "That's not what I said!" or someone said that in response to something you said? Isn't that frustrating? You didn't say what you are being accused of, or you're certain that the other person did say what you think you heard.

"Language is the blood of the soul into which thoughts run and out of which they grow."

— Oliver Wendell Holmes

Everything about language is being filtered through each individual's filter. You may say one thing, meaning one thing, with one intention, but by the time it's flown across the room, or through the airwaves to the other person's ears, you often get responses you never intended or imagined!

This is because your experience is about your experience, not theirs, just as theirs is about them, and not about you.

You have to get through the walls of illusion that are keeping you from understanding that everything in your world is a reflection of the life within you. What you say is a reflection of yourself; what another person says is a reflection of him- or herself.

There are some other interesting things about how human beings work that compound the difficulty of language even more. According to a friend of mine, Les Brown recently gave a talk in which he referred to an MIT study that shows that for every "No" you are told, it will take seventeen "Yeses" to overcome the negativity. I expect this is a result of our egos, which are designed in part to protect us—so they are protecting us from the pain of failure, rejection, etc., when we hear, "No, that will never work" or "No, you can't do that" (in terms of a dream of something) or "No, you aren't talented enough to do that." "You're not being realistic. People like you don't get to do those things," etc. Your ego protects you by programming in, "Okay, we're never going down that road again!" The desire, the dream is stuffed down, deep down, and it takes a lot to pull it back to the surface. A lot of, "Oh, yes you *cans*!"

You are a spark of light. You are filled with ideas and dreams. There are all kinds of things you likely came here to do, be, and become. Perhaps a few of you are focused on one or two specific things, but most people I've spoken to when I ask them what they would love to do, see, be, have, become, etc.—and once they relax and allow themselves to feel their desires—have a long list! But they're rarely working toward any of them. They see most of their list as unattainable.

Why is it that we are so inclined to think our dreams unattainable? What role does language play in our limited thinking?

Language limitations are quite common across cultures. The Dani of New Guinea have only two basic color terms in their language—one for dark colors and one for light colors. (Perhaps everyone is color blind, but I doubt it.) There's a language spoken in North Queensland, Australia, that doesn't have words like left and right or front and back; everything is by direction—east, west, north, south. There are lots of different examples I could cite of limitations in language.

Today, while driving in my car, I noticed that I had my chain yanked by the radio commentator! The DJ on our local radio station reports the weather this way: "Here's the weather situation…." I always jump. To me, when you say there's a "situation," it's alarming! It's not a report. It's not the "current conditions are," it's a "situation"! It's as if he's ringing the alarm bell every time he says it! I'm working on reprogramming my mind not to jump every time I hear him say that.

Here's another example of language's difficulties—this time from a different direction. Have you heard the saying: "Actions speak louder than words"? Have you ever said, "I love you" to someone and had the other person reply, "Actions speak louder than words." I know I heard that as a child if I ventured to say, "I love you" to my mother. I never really knew what to do in response to that. I used to feel crippled because I knew if I tried to "do something" to show my love, I would invariably mess it up. It was never good enough, no matter how hard I tried. Have you ever felt that way?

"In the world I am always a stranger.... I do not understand its language; it does not understand my silence."

— Bei Dao

So for those of us who can relate to this, the whole goal of showing that your actions speak louder than words was an elusive thing that was never achieved. You ended up thinking, "Well, the words will just have to suffice then; I have no actions that are good enough."

How do we communicate effectively? What we are not taught, what is rarely spoken about, is that we are perfectly capable of communicating energetically, psychically, and ethereally.

Case in point, I've been thinking a lot about starting sprouts. We can do so much gardening in our home, but most of us don't take advantage of it. Our local grocery has stopped carrying sprouts because of the problems with various diseases, and I've been hankering for fresh sprouts. I've been thinking about the jars of seeds and the jar-sprouting lids we have, so I made a mental note to dig these things out and get going.

Today as I was doing dishes, I noticed one of the sprouting jars out, assembled, and filled with some seeds. Without ever saying a word to my husband, he had read my mind and started some sprouts. Or perhaps my thoughts about sprouts were a result of me picking up on his thoughts. Either way, it still illustrates my point.

These things have likely happened to you. The only problem is that rather than respecting the mechanism that's working when these things happen, people tend to chalk them up as just coincidences, flukes, or something random that happens. What people don't realize is that every single moment matters. Every single thing that happens and every thought you have matters. Don't be frightened or overwhelmed—it's okay!

Thoughts are energy, just like everything else, so when you think something, it goes out from you like a wave—in many ways, similar to the ripples on a pond when you drop a stone in. It's distinctly different, however, because the ripples on a pond are linear, whereas the energy waves made by thoughts go out from you in *all* directions.

Don't panic! Loving thoughts are logarithmically stronger than thoughts lacking in love, or better put, fearful thoughts. Although, interestingly enough, the lower the frequency, the farther the reach, so low, fearful, and angry thoughts send ripples of energy away from you and travel the farthest, but they have the least amount of force. Higher frequencies don't travel as far, but they are much stronger in force and creative power.

Think about this—there are *only* two states: Love and Lack-of-Love. You may think there are lots of states of mind, but when it comes right down to it, the only true energy is *love*. Anything that appears in form that is not love is only the lack of love. There is nothing else.

Creation, All That Is, is a result of the One Great Mind, Our Shared Parent. That creation is the result of nothing but love, and there is nothing but love—love of our Great Parent, the All That IS. We Are, You Are, I AM, the same One Presence. We are the expression of love, and we are, each of us, the Universe. You are your wildest dream. I am my wildest dream. We all are our Shared Parent's wildest dream!

It is not egotistical to say, *"I am God."* It is not narcissistic. That's not to say that some people are not delusional and confused, and that there are not egotistical, narcissistic maniacs out there declaring that they are God. I am not speaking of that mindset. Those people are confused and have misunderstood the teachings and the way.

You are as much AAH as I am, as any one is. This is the key—we are one, we are WE, united, connected, and whole. No one is superior or better than another. We are all made of the same stuff. We *are* all the same stuff. For every mistake you make while in physical form, for each bad decision, for each wandering away from a place of love, for each of those occurrences, there will be a course correction.

Most of the time, we don't think in pictures but in words, in whatever language we were taught first. I have met people who say they now think in a second or third learned language, but the first language is most common. Sadly, most Americans only know one language.

You are basically what you have thought yourself into being, whether it be with the words, the language you use in your head, or by pictures.

Prince Ea (Richard Williams) has a lovely video he's put together about the labels in language. As he brilliantly summarizes in his video,[17] we are taught to label things from the moment we are born. Society uses labels to describe us, but in doing so, removes our freedom. Labels are limiting, so when children get labeled as slow learners, or troubled youths, or special needs, for example, we are forecasting their future and robbing them of their individual identities.

17 http://www.thisbuzz.com/wow-the-video-thats-taking-the-internet-by-storm-today-will-leave-you-questioning-everything/

"Words hide thoughts, but actions reveal."

— David Armstrong

Sometimes, we find it difficult to hear the truth. Or you may be trying to share your truth with someone you love, but the person is rejecting your offering or suggestion. It hurts, doesn't it? You just want to be seen and heard; witnessed, if you will. It's what we all want. When you feel rejected, you must never take these situations personally. It's important to remember that you can only understand things, within the context of your experience; you only understand to the extent of your character. So it is with everyone. You cannot hear the story of unlimited, infinite love if you do not have these things in your character. The words will fall on deaf ears, as the saying goes. Do not despair—anything lacking can be gained with effort and focus.

If you believe you do have it in your character, but that there are those who are not worthy of love or life, then you do not yet understand the true meaning of unconditional, infinite love. Don't worry! Many people don't. That's what the twenty-first century is all about! That's what this handbook is here to help with—all of us learning how to communicate with each other, outside of the limitations of current, traditional language and circumstances.

You see, our thoughts are waves of energy, so our thoughts are not limited to ourselves. Our thoughts go out into the Unified Field, the All That IS. Our thoughts travel out from us, in our language, but also in the frequency of the thought. The frequency of the thought will match up with the frequency of other thoughts of similar frequency, regardless of the thinker's language.

Like will attract like—they magnetize each other. So if your thoughts are loving, if your thoughts are joyful, if your thoughts are grateful, if your thoughts are expectant of a happy outcome, you will find yourself in a high vibrational frequency, and your experience of life will be seemingly charmed. Even in the face of apparent tragedy, the positive outcome will banish the notion of tragedy.

As we discussed in Chapter 6 of this section, everything around you is listening and participating. When you are joyful, happy, and grateful, everything around you, every single atom that surrounds you, rides the waves of your high frequency and is attracted to you and attracts more of the same to you and it.

If, however, your thoughts are unhappy, your thoughts are of what you are lacking, your thoughts are ungrateful, your thoughts are mean, your thoughts are angry, your thoughts are obsessed with the wrongs that have been done to you, or about what someone said or did to you, then everything around you hears and feels that and vibrates to that lower, lacking in spirit, energy.

Often, you can tell what someone is thinking or how someone is feeling by what we refer to as body language. Here's yet another form of communication or language! If you are standing or sitting with your arms crossed, it would be generally accepted that you are in a defensive posture, un-open to what's being said. You are protecting yourself from attack. It may also mean you are not interested in what you are hearing, or in the person who is speaking.

If, instead, your arms are open, then you are open to what you are hearing, or you are interested in what is being said. If you are leaning in, you are especially interested; leaning back, you are extra interested in increasing your distance from the subject or person.

> *"I've learned that people may forget what you said, people will forget what you did, but they will never forget how you made them feel."*
>
> *—Maya Angelou*

It would be nice if we could communicate like cats, for example. A cat uses its tail to communicate how it's feeling:

- An arched back and inflated tail means it's angry or defensive.
- A flat back and an inflated tail means it's afraid (which is quiet often proceeded by a jump in the air.
- A tail straight up means it's happy to see you.
- A tail straight up and wagging means it's ecstatic to see you.
- A tail straight up with a curling tip means it's friendly.
- A tail drooped between its legs means it's concerned.
- If its tail is swishing back and forth seductively, well, you know.
- If the tail is down and it's flicking the tip, then the cat is irritated.

Just like a cat, you can tell when someone is irritated with you, can't you? Even if the person never says a word. Really, you can tell when someone is any of those qualities like the cat above. You can tell even more. You can tell when someone is annoyed, impatient, fed up, agitated; you can tell when someone is being judgmental, or when someone is bullying you with just his or her posture.

How do you feel then? You feel like the beaten cat or dog, don't you? With your tail between your legs. You want to curl up into a ball and cry. That's our ultimate protection, when we curl into a ball, we're protecting all our soft parts. We need our soft parts.

Often, when we're experiencing the pain of life, it hurts us in our stomach or belly. You actually have three brain centers in your body: Your brain is one brain center, your heart is a brain center, and your belly or gut is a brain center. Haven't you ever felt something in your gut? It's what is called a gut feeling—when you know something is wrong.

Language is limited. When you experience life to the extent that is intended by the All That IS, you will be left speechless; you will be without words and in a state of awe that transcends anything we have in the English language.

There is a word in Japanese/Chinese culture, *yũgen*, that means something like a deep, profound, perhaps infinite awareness of the universe, that triggers emotional responses too deep and mysterious for words. Its exact usage depends upon the context, so an exact translation is difficult.

> *"Language is clumsy, understanding is subjective, religion is obstructive. We must rise above these obstacles to achieve complete being."*
>
> *— Kate Miler*

Language is a pervasive wall, and you will have to work diligently to keep on top of what you are saying and what you really intend to say or communicate. Being mindful of your speech is one of the most important takeaways I can give you. Realizing everything is listening should help you remember that the words you use are important. Thoughts and spoken words are things. They carry a vibrational frequency, which means they permeate all that surrounds you.

If you go around swearing all the time, then everything around you is shriveling and cringing. If you say, "That will never happen," or "They'll never do that," or "That's not possible," then the Universe and All That IS hears that and withdraws from the flow, interpreting your declarations as if you do not want these things.

When you say you *can't* do something, everything hears you, and because all that surrounds you is trying to give you what you want, and since you are saying you can't, then you will receive what you are declaring you want...which is that you can't.

"Whether you think you can,
or you think you can't, you're right."

— Henry Ford

Many people, when they begin these studies, will shift from complaining about not having something, to saying, "It is on its way to me." That is certainly an improvement, but still what you are creating is experience of the thing being on the way to you, rather than with you. You are not creating the experience of having it, whatever it may be, but still creating the experience of it being elusive and on the way.

When you fully grasp the concept, you understand that you must say, "I have," and "I am," even before you have, or are, that thing. Then you are being the creative being you are intended to be. When you declare you are something, even before you are that thing, all that surrounds you and supports you realizes what you want, and if you are not yet at the frequency of having it, everything works to fill the river of flow to you. Becoming whatever it is you wish to become will be easier to achieve; the way will open up for you. This is something the great Muhammad Ali understood. His life is a great demonstration of these principles.

> *"It's the repetition of affirmations that leads to belief. And once that belief becomes a deep conviction, things begin to happen."*
>
> *— Muhammad Ali*

The Universe, the All That IS, the AAH, is supporting you, opening up the way for you. Help is always available to you. Very few seem to know this—hence, this handbook. People need to know!

Help is always available; you are not alone. I know you feel alone, but you are not. You are surrounded by loving, conscious, substance that wants nothing more than for you to feel joy, to be happy, to know bliss. You are AAH in physical expression. Why would the One Great Mind, the All That IS, desire anything or create anything other than joy for itself?

The density of energy here on Earth/Gaia/Eden is really strong. It's extremely difficult to get connected with Source, harder still to stay connected. When you connect, you connect to this flow of love of which I speak. Even during the darkest times of my life, my life was orchestrated so that I always ended up in the right place and things always worked out for the best.

Learning to become mindful of what you say, not just out loud, but also to yourself, in your head, is one of the most important things you can do to help bring yourself back into connection with flow and All That IS. Do you say things like, "I could never do that," about things you would really like to do? Or "That will never happen." "I should have...." "I can't...." "I'll never...." "I'm so dumb...." Or "I always do that" (about something you'd prefer not to do)?

Everything is listening, but nothing understands complaining. Everything understands the language being used, the language heard. Nothing understand the subtlety underlying the words. Therefore, when you say any of the phrases above, or anything else along those lines, what everything surrounding you hears is you wanting these things.

Abracadabra: I create as I speak. Or as I speak, I create.

In Volumes II and III, I will go into language again in depth in the areas of both love and health. Our language and self-talk play one of the largest roles in creating reality. It is true that you get what you ask for. The problem is you don't understand that you are asking! For that reason, you *do* always do that thing you really wish you didn't do, and you are so dumb, and you can't do whatever it is you wish you could, and it won't ever happen, and you won't ever have whatever, and on and on it goes.

We tend to go through life complaining about the things we don't have, and by doing so, we are actually increasing our lack! If, instead, you adopt an attitude of abundance and unlimited possibility, and you allow that attitude to be reflected in your language, you actually create the energetic flow for everything you want to flow to you.

Of course, changing the language you use can seem overwhelming. You need to be gentle with yourself and understand that change of this kind takes time (and since we know there's no such thing as time, your desired outcome already exists). Watch yourself and your words. Your focus on being mindful will make it easier to catch yourself and restate your words with the intent you choose.

I have no monetary connection to this book, but everyone on the planet should get a copy of *The Comfort Coloring Book*. It is filled with the principles of self-care, self-love, and love in general that I am sharing with you in these volumes. In a very beautiful way, this coloring book uses loving and inspiring quotes interwoven in the drawings—the author makes the wonderful suggestion of coloring on your lunch break. What a fantastic idea! Combining inspiring language with the meditative quality of coloring.

In any case, my point here is that we really must watch our words—take care in what we say. A great tool is to tape up 3x5 cards everywhere with positive phrases and/or carry a small notebook with positive phrases that you can read throughout the day. It takes focus, time, attention, and effort. At first, you will find that your ego will fight you. You will find excuses for not doing these exercises. Find someone who shares your interest; support each other in these lessons.

Lose the word "never." Memorize the phrase, "Never say never." It's a serious thing. Any time you catch yourself saying "never," remind yourself to never say never, and then repeat the statement in a positive way. If people question you, just say you are learning to be more positive.

When you are tempted to say to someone, "You never pick up your room," or "You never do the dishes," or "You never say you love me," remember that you are creating more of what you are declaring. If this result is not what you are after, change your words!

Take the above examples and turn them around by taking responsibility for your feelings and needs. What is it you are trying to accomplish? How about, "I could really use help with the dishes." "It's important to me that you pick up your room." "I would really appreciate it if you would tell me you love me more often than you do." Own your truth; learn to speak your truth.

If you are not already, you need to learn to be responsible for your language. Own what you are saying. The world is a reflection of you, to you. When you point your finger outward and blame those around you, or the situation around you, for your circumstance and experience, you are giving all your power away, and you are being delusional at the same time. As the saying goes, "There may be one finger pointing out, but there's three fingers pointed back at you."

When we have not yet done our inner work, we think that what's wrong is external, and we point our finger around and complain. We'll talk about this in great detail in Volume II, and I'll give you lots of tools for working through this wall.

You can start on this right away, though, by employing one of the commandments my mother taught me: "If you can't say anything nice, don't say anything at all!" There is more wisdom in that saying than many realize. It's not just about not complaining, and it's not just about being nice. It's about *everything is listening*!

I'll take it even further. Not only is everything listening, but everything is willing and able to communicate with us, too.

Sure, it may sound crazy, but it's not; trust me. When you tune into the energy around yourself, when you function at the frequency of love and above, you'll discover that everything is communicating with you. When you need a certain tool, it will magically appear; when you need to get someplace on time, you'll do it, even after spending extra time in a traffic jam or waiting on a broken-down train. You'll miss a plane, train, ride, etc., only to dodge some tragedy, all because someone stopped you to ask a question. It also works the same way—things will disappear just when you need them and show back up after the need is gone. This is a case of the thing itself not wanting to participate in whatever was going to happen. Yes, it sounds crazy, but really, start paying attention. You'll see.

Have you ever known someone who is always breaking things, or is always losing things, or perhaps can't hold a job? Everything is energy in these and all cases. What is happening is a reflection of the prevailing energy. So if your energy, and your words, your language, is one of fear, or despair, or anger, or depression, then everything around you is going to want to get away from your energetic field. Everything around you is shrinking back into itself; you have cut yourself off from flow because in your state of mind, you have created a wall around yourself through which little can penetrate. Everything is horrible, or terrible, or difficult, or challenging; therefore, everything provides exactly that.

Everything is life, and all life can feel your energy. Since all life is connected and a part of the Great Shared Parent, everything IS AAH in physical expression. When you state your displeasure with the life you find yourself having, everything around you feels that rejection. You are rejecting the gift of life.

Have you heard, "Be careful what you ask for"? This is another important and sage piece of wisdom that doesn't get enough attention in our upbringing.

"'Should' is a bad place to live, but boy,
do we set up a lot of tents there."

— Saul Bass

Everything around you is doing all that it can to support you, but you really need to stay focused on the question, "What is it that I am going to do that fulfills me, that is also going to be best for the good of the whole. What is *my* gift that I came here to share?"

You need to come first, then after that, family, then friends, then the whole world, because you are a part of the whole world. You are a part of All That IS—you are All That IS—so you need to take care of yourself first. Honor yourself. Speak kindly to yourself. Learn the language of self-love. Get comfortable saying, "I am whole, perfect, strong, powerful, loving, harmonious, and happy."

Reaffirm to yourself that you are stardust. You are part of the Universe. The Universe is in you! You are a magnificent, amazing being.

What challenges can you identify in your pattern of speech and thought that can use some focus and adjustment?

1)

2)

3)

4)

5)

"The limits of my language mean the limits of my world."

— Ludwig Wittgenstein

Chapter 9

GETTING OUT OF YOUR OWN WAY

"You had a purpose before anyone had an opinion."

— Unknown

Just as the first wall was yourself, the last wall is also yourself; both what you believe about yourself and what you believe about what others tell you about yourself.

We have a tendency to cling to what is familiar—even when what is familiar is causing unhappiness or discomfort in our lives.

"Time is the substance from which I am made. Time is a river which carries me along, but I am the river; it is a tiger which devours me, but I am the tiger; it is a fire that consumes me, but I am the fire."

— Jorge Luis Borges

While we can't blame other people or circumstances for how we are feeling because we can take control of our feelings, we do tend to stay in situations and circumstances that don't result in pleasant feelings. One of the reasons we stay in the unpleasant situations we are in is because we are afraid of the unknown. What we know is more comforting than the unknown, even if the unknown might look better to us. Human beings are, by nature, creatures of comfort.

We see this with abused women all the time. They will return to the battering home, not because they want to, but because they don't know what would become of them if they didn't. Their identity has become that of a battered woman. For that reason, they can't see the way out—there is, in essence, no way out. They are trapped by their beliefs, by their identities.

So one of the first things you'll need to do, now that you have walked through all the other walls, is to walk through yourself.

"Just because you got the monkey off your back doesn't mean the circus has left town."

— George Carlin

Walk yourself to a new world, to the world you imagine is possible—to the world you see other people living but can't seem to find for yourself. Walk yourself to the world where life flows easily and you feel deeply rich and fulfilled, loved and appreciated.

"Get out of your own way...stop the paralysis by analysis...decide what you want, create a simple plan, and get moving!"

— Steve Maraboli

Walk yourself to a new world where you are healthy from the inside out, where you are connected with the abundant flow of energy from Source—where you feel vibrant and alive.

How do you get out of your own way? Well, that's what the next volumes are dedicated to: the tools you need to walk through yourself to the real you, the you that's been waiting for you to find it, the you that's been waiting to be seen, the you that's just waiting to emerge and take life, the you that you've always dreamed of, the you of unlimited possibilities and greatness for the good of all, the you of the gifts you came here to share.

I want you to know that I am here for you. Reach out to me if you need support as you are walking through these walls! I'm here to help you with this process. I'm here to help you implement and integrate these steps and the results you'll achieve!

"You've gotta find a way to get out of your own way, so you can progress in life."

— Steve Carlton

Can you think of ways that you are in your own way? Do you do things that sabotage your efforts?

1)

2)

3)

4)

5)

"In the end only three things matter. How much you loved, how gently you lived, and how gracefully you let go of things not meant for you."

— Buddha

SUMMARY OF VOLUME I

Summary of Volume I

THE SECRET WALL

"Time is the coin of your life. It is the only coin you have, and only you can determine how it will be spent. Be careful lest you let other people spend it for you."

— Carl Sandburg

It is important to me that this handbook be easy to hold, comfortable in your hand, and not so heavy that you don't want to carry it around. Hence, due to the length of this entire handbook, as you know, it is broken into three volumes.

I hope that in this first volume you got a good introduction to the life of humanity, to our purpose, to your purpose, and to the challenges we face in this third dimension.

In the supplement section following, I give you seven tools you can start with, or add, to your regime of awakening.

If I've illuminated things clearly, you now realize that life, all of life, is of your own making. Your life is a reflection of what you look for. Life shows up for us in the manner we expect. In fact, the only reason we see anything at all is because we go looking for it. By looking for it, you magnetize your frequency, what you think about, and what you go looking for. You get what you give. You create what you think about, and you become what you think about most of the time.

"You are now, and you do become, what you think about."

— Earl Nightingale

You also realize that what others say to you, or about you, is a reflection of them—a reflection of who they are on the inside, and a reflection of who they think you are. What they say is not a true reflection of you. It is a true reflection of them.

Only you truly can know who you are. You know this from looking within yourself, not looking outward and taking in what other people say about you. If you have not yet done so, now is the time to take charge of yourself and start.

"To simply wake up every morning a
better person than when I went to bed."

— Sidney Poitier

Remember what Don Miguel Ruiz teaches us about others: 1) Don't take anything personally, and 2) Never make assumptions.

Another important thing to realize is that when you change your expectations, when you let go of your requirements and prejudices, all of nature and the energy of the Universe will push forth to aid you on your way. Remember, everything is participating in this illusion we call life; when you embrace life at the level of which I am speaking, everything knows, and everything around you will support you in your life.

When you have the faith that you are safe, that you are in good hands, that you have help always available to you, then the entire Universe is at your service and you will experience miracles daily. The key here is having faith. I can give personal testimony about how having faith first, blind faith if you will, yields the greatest magic ever. Many people mistakenly think that they will learn faith through experiences, when, in fact, it is through faith that we experience miracles.

I know personally that every time I have "laid down the law" to AAH and asked for a sign, asked for help, my call has been answered. I recall a quite striking time when I was thirteen; I made a promise to AAH that if AAH brought me back my lost dog, I would believe in AAH forever. I was bereft without my dog. He was my world, in what could only be described as a miserable existence. I was unhappy beyond words. Later that day, the phone rang. It was our vet calling because someone had brought the dog in and the vet recognized him. (This was long before microchipping, and it truly was a miracle. The people lived thirty miles away. The odds of them taking this dog to our vet were really low.) Unbelievably, I had my dog back by nightfall. Whenever I have fallen into disconnection and begun to question whether there is such a thing as a Great Parent, or question the existence of AAH, I have remembered my promise always to believe if I were given my dog back. My call for help was answered with a miracle; it only takes my remembering for it to happen again. Every call I have ever made has been answered, and so it will be with you, when you believe.

All that we know in life, truly know, we know through our experience, our own experience—not anyone else's. Sure, we can know things intellectually, and we can listen to other people's stories, but to know something truly, to understand something intimately, you must know it through personal experience. For example, I can tell you all there is to know about time and synchronicity and everything being an illusion, but it is my experience of the disappearing scarf that showed me it's true.

The secret wall that few realize exists is the wall of faith. Now that you know the walls, now that you know that life is this crazy illusion that you control with your reactions, the final piece you need to know is that you must believe. You must believe that all is possible; you must believe that all is always well, regardless of appearances. You must believe that everything will always work out for the best, regardless of apparent difficulty.

Having that level of faith will speed you along your way. I promise you this.

"Ships don't sink because of the water around them; ships sink because of the water that gets in them. Don't let what's around you get inside and weigh you down."

— Unknown

If you have stayed with me to this end, I am deeply honored and grateful for your attention. I apologize in advance if you will be delayed in continuing on with Volume II or III because they are not yet out. I am writing as quickly as I can. I embrace you as very special because you are one of my first readers!

As you may recall from the Preface, Volume II will pick up where we leave off here, starting with The Tools of Life, where I will take you through all the tools you have available to you in life to help you get the most out of life and live your life to the fullest.

In the next section, The Way to Love, we'll go through using the tools and applying them in daily living to find love for yourself, and then for everyone else.

Volume II is packed with help for sorting out and navigating life and should offer transformative tips for many.

Volume III will start with The Way to Health, and then takes everything you will have learned from Volumes I and II and shows you how to move the concepts out into the world. Now that you've healed your life and found love for yourself and others, and you've found health, you'll be ready to start walking your love and understanding out into the world around you. Volume III gives you the structure for bringing all the lessons of mindfulness, peace, love, and oneness into your daily life—and the daily lives of those around you.

The world is ready for a new direction; there is a call for a new way to govern and a new way to move commerce through creativity rather than competition. There are lots of ideas. There isn't yet the structure for cohesion and unification of effort. I'm hoping this handbook will help provide the guidelines for cohesion and unification of effort.

It's true that it takes each one of us working together as a part of a greater whole. We are one humanity, if you will, spinning around on this globe of water and dirt in the middle of a solar system, in the middle of a galaxy, in the middle of a nebula, and on and on it goes, into the unending universe of space.

We are in this thing called life together, and we are on this thing (Earth/Gaia/Eden) together. Technology allows us to connect with each other around the world, so we can use it until we all figure out how to access the Unified Field and connect, as we already are, on other planes.

Ultimately, we are all one; we are all connected, and with practice, we can connect in the ether. We don't need the technology. We don't need Facebook or cell phones or the Internet. When we finally learn who we are, when you finally learn who you are, you won't need the newscaster to tell you something has happened. You'll know it already. You might know it ahead of time, if need be.

You are an amazing being, made from stardust and governed, guided, and beloved by a force larger than anything you can likely imagine. I have seen it for myself in action. Because I have seen it, I know that everything I say is true. Unless you believe something is possible, you will never see it. You have to believe in miracles in order to witness miracles.

I know I am likely leaving you with many unanswered questions, but I am not really leaving you. I want you to feel free to contact me via email, website, or phone. I am not abandoning you. I am here for you.

So until we meet again in the pages of the next volume, I challenge you to believe. Believe it is possible—whatever your wildest dreams may be—as long as they are for the best good you, and the good of the whole, believe you can achieve them. Then each day do all you can to move forward toward your dreams. If your dreams are something that contributes to the greater good of all, and you are in harmony with All That IS, living your gift, you will become unstoppable.

Use the tools I have given you thus far and in the supplement, and you will go far with these alone, even before Volume II is available!

Believe it possible. Act with faith and purpose. You achieve what you believe. If you find you are struggling, there is a good chance you are dealing with an underlying contradictory belief. Such beliefs often come from your childhood. Remember the seventeen yeses you need to overcome the one no. Remember that people are a reflection of themselves, not of you. You need to find the *you* within you. The real you, the you that you choose to create—not the you that you have been told you are, or told to create to please others.

No one knows you better than you. Figure out who you are. Believe you can, and believe you make a difference. You do. Perhaps you make all the difference.

"Remember that your natural state is joy."

— Wayne Dyer

Supplement

PUTTING KNOWLEDGE INTO PRACTICE

Supplement

PUTTING KNOWLEDGE INTO PRACTICE

Preview of Future Volumes

"We must return to the roots of our ancestors and honor the spiritual nature of our physical universe (... the lesson offered by quantum physics!). In order to get there, we must first recognize and honor the fact that each of us is a spiritual entity inhabiting a physical body. Honoring is the foundation of harmony."

— Bruce Lipton, Ph.D.

When I set out to write this handbook, I had no idea it would be so many pages that it would need to be broken down into three volumes. It's difficult to ask you to stop here. I'm finding it difficult myself to part from you. To just end things now seems so abrupt.

In Volume I of this handbook, we've covered a lot of ground—mostly a lot of history and science. I don't feel comfortable wrapping this volume up without at least giving you some tools, in an organized manner, to start you on the process of walking through your walls. Volume II has a long chapter on The Tools and lists almost every tool under the sun. This supplement is a primer to get you started.

Since the entire handbook encompasses an overview of the seven chakra system, I am going to leave you with a tool for each chakra so you can begin, if you haven't already, to open the flow between your different energy centers—and get yourself humming, so to speak.

When all seven of your chakras are open and flowing, it allows the energy of life to flow through you unimpeded, and this is when the real magic starts to happen. You are, if you remember, AAH in physical expression. You are a creation of Creation, and you are not only a creator yourself, but you are connected to all of Creation. Your powers, when used for the good of the whole, are unlimited. But you cannot achieve your unlimited potential when you are blocked energetically or vibrating at a low frequency.

To get started, here are some very simple but extremely powerful tools that will give you immediate and sustaining results, when applied consistently, for living consciously and opening up your flow of energy and connection to Source and the All That IS.

- Sitting Quietly and Getting to Know Yourself — Root Chakra
- Learning How to Breathe — Sacral Chakra
- Learning to Control Your Thoughts — Solar Plexus Chakra
- Adhering to The Four Agreements — Heart Chakra
- Learning to Control Your Words — Throat Chakra
- Starting Your Day with a Writing Exercise — Third Eye Chakra
- Intending Your Life with WE LOVE US — Crown Chakra

Don't be overwhelmed by this list. Start with breathing and take it at whatever pace works for you. Change is change—it takes some getting used to. As you change, others will be affected. Be patient with yourself and others. Give yourself compassion and love. Forgive yourself for forgetting you are divine. You can do this. It's called waking up.

"Enter through the narrow gate. For wide is the gate and broad is the road that leads to destruction, and many enter through it. But small is the gate and narrow the road that leads to life, and only a few find it."

— Matthew 7:13-14

Supplement 1

SITTING QUIETLY AND GETTING TO KNOW YOURSELF — ROOT CHAKRA

"Finding some quiet time in your life,
I think, is hugely important."

— Mariel Hemingway

The way you find out who you are is you sit quietly. This can be called meditation, mindfulness, or just sitting quietly. If you never sit quietly, you can never hear what your Spirit and the Universe or Source is trying to say to you. You are Source in physical expression—in a meat suit if you will. AAH is inhabiting this meat suit with you; you are in this together. If you never sit quietly, you may never discover your connection.

"Listen—are you breathing just a little,
and calling it a life?"

— Mary Oliver

In this third dimension, a human body is what you, in your divine expression, inhabit. You are not your body. Your body is where you live in third dimension, but this is not real. We've covered this. The third dimension is an illusion. You exist beyond your physical form!

The only way you are going to get in touch with that formless self, the you that is the eternal spirit in expression in your physical form, is to sit quietly. You can do this easily, just by starting. Take an extra few minutes in the car when you arrive somewhere, or a few extra minutes sitting on the side of your bed before you get up and start your day—a few minutes in the bathroom even. Find some place you feel comfortable and safe and make the time. Start with just five minutes if you are pressed for time; start with one minute if that's all you can manage. As you do this, it will grow on you and you will begin to seek out more time—longer and more often. These times will become your haven. Trust me on this. It may seem rough going to start, but let me assure you, with every fiber of my being, this truly is the most important thing you can do. If you do nothing else, do this. Connect with yourself by sitting quietly—learn who you are.

Make sure you are comfortable in whatever you are wearing. Loosen any restrictive clothing. Sit comfortably—I believe your intention and focus is more important than your posture.

You will have to play around with what works for you with your eyes. I close my eyes, but often, closed eyes will make for a busy mind, or if you are tired, you may fall asleep. Open eyes locked on a focal point is one popular method, and this works well because if you keep your eyes locked and focus on your breath, it's the easiest way to keep your mind from wandering. Focusing on something with the idea of not taking your eyes off of it (like a candle or a photo or painting, or some other focal point), combined with focus on your breathing causes a very strong use of the right side of your brain, keeping left brain activity at bay at least, so you're 50 percent of the way there! Ha ha! Another method is to have your eyes partially open and out of focus. This tends to be what Buddhist monks practice.

Then just focus on your breath. As you breathe, focus on the breath coming in, moving down to your core, through all seven of your chakras down to your root, and then back up. Consider how as you breathe you are drawing in life. Realize that your breath is your life. As you breathe, you fill each cell of your body with life-giving oxygen. It is each breath you take that keeps you alive. It's not the food you eat or the water you drink—it's the air you breathe. Honor it, bless it, be grateful for what it empowers you with, which is everything. It empowers you with life. Without it, you will be nothing in physical form because your meat suit will cease to function. Without your breath, you, the you that is real, the you that exists beyond time and space, will return to the whole. Without your breath, you will leave your third-dimension body behind.

Through your breath, as you breathe, you can learn to connect not only to yourself, but to the whole, the All That IS, while still in your meat suit, while still in this third dimension. Doesn't that sound like a good idea—to connect with the greater vision, the larger plan, to connect with your reason for being here in this meat suit?

As you breathe, give yourself love; appreciate the miracle that is you. You are a unique expression in physical form; trillions of cells are all working together to create your body suit—a child of the One Great Mind, the All That IS. Tune into your body. Quiet your mind and listen—listen to what your body and spirit want to tell you. Quiet yourself and allow the Great Parent to speak to you.

When you start this practice, you may discover that your body wants to fight you. You may feel the need to cough or scratch. You may find yourself fidgeting or find it difficult to get comfortable. Sitting quietly will become a battle with your body as you test the length of time you can sit. You may find your eyes will water, or your nose will suddenly start running. It will take a great effort on your part to resist these urges. If you are meditating in a group, sometimes this can be the result of group energy, but more likely, it is your ego fighting you for control of the situation.

Your ego is here to protect you and keep you safe, but your ego thinks it is in control of you. If you are new to mindfulness, your ego thinks that it is in control of your mind and your body. Your ego is frightened to let go.

"The key to change...is to let go of fear."

— Rosanne Cash

When you choose to sit (or lie) quietly and be mindful, your ego freaks out. (I don't suggest lying, unless you are doing a guided meditation because the risk of falling asleep is much higher. This practice is not about sleeping.) Your ego fights for control by trying to make you itch, or cough, or move; it twitches, your eyes will water, your nose will run.... You get the idea! It's a struggle, but it's important you take control. It's important to resist the impulse to move, cough, scratch, etc. Let the tears run down your cheek. Observe them in a detached manner. Do not give in to wiping them. I am good at fighting everything except a runny nose. If that happens,

I have to give in and get a tissue. (Always have a tissue in a pocket or within reach, just in case.) It is true that when our eyes water, our nose will also run.

Sit comfortably, focus, blur, or close your eyes, and pay attention to nothing but your breath. Feel your body moving as you breathe. Try to draw your breath all the way to your lower belly. Find a comfortable position for your hands. As your mind wanders, just bring your attention back to your breath.

Just sit quietly and focus on your breath; as thoughts come, observe them, but let them go and bring your attention back to your breath. Wayne Dwyer suggested you are trying to get "into the gap"—the space between one thought and the next, and by doing so, you make conscious contact with the creative energy of life itself.

Do not get frustrated; be loving and forgiving with yourself. When you first start this practice, your mind will be very busy, most likely. As you practice sitting quietly, the struggle with your ego will make itself apparent, but it will get easier, and eventually, it will go away. You will have gained control. It will take some time. Be patient and forgiving with yourself. It's a practice. It's not a doing—it's a practice. You learn and grow. It's an exploration in being. It's a discovery of self.

"I have learned, that the person I have to ask for forgiveness from the most is: myself. You must love yourself. You have to forgive yourself, every day, whenever you remember a shortcoming, a flaw, you have to tell yourself 'That's just fine.' You have to forgive yourself so much, until you don't even see those things anymore. Because that's what love is like."

— C. JoyBell C.

You are on a beautiful journey into becoming. You are starting the process of awakening and walking through your walls. You most likely have a lot to unlearn. You've quite possibly been led astray. You've been told to be afraid—to live in fear; to honor something or someone outside of yourself.

In reality, it all starts within. The answers are within. The truth is within. Everything you need to know about you, who you are, what your life is supposed to be and become, it all comes from within. If you never listen, if you never learn how to hear, you will likely miss out on the miracles just waiting to emerge for you.

I know that what I am suggesting here may seem terrifying to you. Remember this: I am holding your hand on your journey. If you feel lost, or overwhelmed, just close your eyes and connect with me energetically—know that I am here to support you, and I believe in you. And I know you can do this. I have done it myself, and I know anyone can do this. You are stronger than you can imagine. When you keep your focus on yourself and fulfilling your life purpose, and when your purpose is for the good of the whole (not the development of yourself for selfish reasons), you cannot fail once you get on your path. Everything in the universe will support you.

"The best remedy for those who are afraid, lonely, or unhappy is to go outside, somewhere where they can be quiet, alone with the heavens, nature, and God. Because only then does one feel that all is as it should be."

— Anne Frank

Supplement 2

LEARNING HOW TO BREATHE — SACRAL CHAKRA

"For breath is life, and if you breathe well, you will live long on earth."

— Sanskrit Proverb

Life starts and ends with our breath. When we are born, we breathe from our lower bellies. If you watch babies sleeping on their backs, their chests do not go up and down. Their lower bellies go up and down, as they breathe. This lower belly breathing is one of the connections to the area of the seat of our soul and our connection to our Great Parent and All That IS, the One Mind. It is a visual indication of our connection to our toroidal energy matrix.

When you breathe, ideally you will draw the energy of the breath all the way down your chakra system to your root chakra, and when you exhale, the breath energetically comes all the way from your root—up, up, up, through all the chakras, and energetically leaves through the crown chakra on the top of your head.[18]

As we age, usually around age two, our breath starts to become more and more shallow, eventually for most, settling in the chest. This is most likely the effect of the fear imprint around us. As we grow up, unless we are able to counteract the influence of collective fear, we will become more and more fearful, and our breath will become more and more shallow, and higher in our chests. The constrictions come as we clench our guts; the more fearful we are, the farther up our torso the clenching reaches. Extremely fearful people, and perhaps children living among extremely fearful people, are very shallow breathers.

When this clenching happens, then energetically, you and your chakras, your energy centers, are also going to be blocked because you are not drawing the energy of life all the way down to your root. This is the beginning of our disconnection from Source. Breath is life. Without it, we perish, and yet we pay little regard to how we breathe. We don't have classes on breathing. It's not part of any typical school curriculum that I'm aware of (outside of yoga and other related studies). Learning to breathe so that you are connecting to the Life of the whole, to the power of the Universe, to the eternal life within you, to the All That IS, to AAH, is not taught as a matter of course, and herein lies the problem.

When polled, 80 percent of a room full of people will usually say their chests, upper chests, moved when they breathed, as

---

18 In Volume II, I will introduce you to an advanced breathing technique that starts by you drawing the breath up from the earth, thereby reversing the direction of the travel through your chakras.

opposed to their middles or lower bellies. It's been my experience that breathing will break down into those three regions.

Learning how to breathe properly is one of the most important things you can do if you want to connect with yourself, as you have begun to do by sitting quietly. Breathing into your lower belly is a great way to begin or augment your self-study. It also will lead to greater things—combined with sitting quietly, it will lead to things beyond your wildest dreams.

Begin by getting comfortable. It's nice if you can be sitting in a chair with your feet flat on the floor. I believe once you enter into the mindset of connection and oneness, everything around you knows it and picks up on the vibration, and the experience will be just as powerful in any position. The only challenge is with the visualization of the toroidal energy flowing.

Make sure you are comfortable, and then as you breathe in, visualize the thread of energy coming down from the toroidal energy field around earth, down to you, passing through your core, through all of your energy centers, Crown, Third Eye, Throat, Heart, Solar Plexus, Sacral, Root, down your legs, into the earth, and then as you exhale, it wraps back up, around your body, back up to your crown chakra, meeting up with the flow from above, and wrapping again into your crown as you inhale, and passing downward through your chakras, back to the Earth, exhaling, wrapping around and returning, again and again, and as you visualize this, seeing the energy flowing, breathe, not to inflate the lungs, but to draw the breath, in, in, in, down, down, down until your belly expands; do this to a count of seven. Hold for a count of seven—then exhale to a count of seven. Repeat.

Spend as much time practicing lower belly breathing and visualizing the toroidal energy flow as you can. Each time you do, you will be increasing your connection to your power center. You will be opening up the flow of energy to your chakras. And you will be connecting to Source. You can practice this visualization and breathing while in the shower.

You can augment this practice with a standing position combined with arm movements, which will assist in clearing your energy field. Start with your feet about shoulder-width apart so you are stable. Keeping your arms straight and at your sides, bring the back of your hands together. As you inhale, draw your hands up, your center up, up, over your head, keeping the backs of your hands together, at the top, splitting; then as you exhale, bring your arms down while keeping them out, turning your palms down as they lower; bring the backs of your hands together; inhale and repeat the process. Look on the website WalkingThroughYourWalls.com for an example of this breathing pose and technique.

You may have heard the recommendation, "When you get upset, breathe." If you learn to lower belly breathe, and apply that when you get upset, you'll find a new world will open to you—and quickly. When you find yourself upset, tune into your breathing; bring your focus to your breath, and allow yourself to become calm by breathing into your lower belly. It will serve you better than just counting to ten.

"Feelings come and go like clouds in a windy sky.
Conscious breathing is my anchor."

— Thích Nhat Hanh

Supplement 3

LEARNING TO CONTROL YOUR THOUGHTS — SOLAR PLEXUS CHAKRA

"The most difficult thing is the decision to act, the rest is merely tenacity. The fears are paper tigers. You can do anything you decide to do. You can act to change and control your life; and the procedure, the process is its own reward."

— *Amelia Earhart*

Learn to control your thoughts. You can easily do this. (Although at first it will feel like a struggle, if you can persevere the first few days or a week, you *will* learn to do this!) Pick a good solid mantra[19] or short saying.

19 If you want to use something other than the ten words I use, your own custom mantra, please be sure it is 100 percent positive. You can feel free to email me. There is also a resource at www.WalkingThroughYourWalls.com to use to check the power of your intentions. You want to be careful you are magnetizing to you what you want, not what you don't want.

I chose:

> "I am whole, perfect, strong, powerful, loving, harmonious, and happy." (From *The Secret* by Rhonda Byrne.)

Those are my ten little words, as I like to call them. You have no idea how many people will say, "Oh, I could never learn that, memorize that." Never say never. You *can* do this. And if you set your mind to it, you can do anything good you set your mind to.

"The mind is everything. What you think, you become."

— Buddha

I bought some of those business cards you can run through a printer and I designed them with the ten words on one side and on the reverse I put the following (also from *The Secret*):

I AM God in a physical body.

I AM Spirit in the flesh.

I AM Eternal life expressing itself as me.

I AM all powerful, all intelligence.

I AM wisdom.

I AM perfection.

I AM the Creator,

Creating the creation

Of Me, on this planet.

You can use anything to make these cards—use index cards or make your own out of whatever you have handy. If you have to handwrite them, then handwrite them. If you have old business cards that you can write on the back side of, use those. If you can laminate them so they last, all the better! The point is to take action!

"You must not ever stop being whimsical. And you must not, ever, give anyone else the responsibility for your life."

— Mary Oliver

Take these cards and put them everywhere. Tape one to the mirror in your bathroom, one to your dashboard, and one to your computer monitor. Put them in the pockets of your jackets, coats, sweaters—put them in your pants, purses, backpacks. Slip one in your wallet, in your ID sleeve, in your credit card or phone case. Having them and seeing them everywhere will help imprint upon your memory your intent to learn to control your mind and thoughts. Some people will write on their hands or arms. I am not suggesting this, but I can't stop you! Find what works and stick with it!

Start with the ten words, or the mantra of your choice, and memorize them. Then, whenever your mind is wandering around aimlessly in your head, when you notice it's wandered off to something non-productive, sad, maddening, etc., repeat your words or mantra. Try to keep your mind in the present, and use the ten words or mantra of your choice as your focus. As you are walking, repeat it in rhythm to your pace. It's a way to meditate while going about your day. Set the words to a tune and sing them silently in your head, or out loud in your car, or in the shower—sing while exercising, gardening, washing dishes, etc. The moment you realize you are thinking about anything other than being in the moment, go back to your words or mantra statement.

When you get bored with the short mantra, you can memorize the flip side of the card or the longer poem. Set it to music. Alternate the use of the two sides. But above all, learn to keep your thoughts at home. Do not spend time thinking about other people and what they have said and done to you or anyone else. Do not think about what other people should be doing at all. Mind your own business. Focus on becoming the best you that you can be. Forget everyone else. Everyone else's life purpose is not your business. If you are a parent, this applies to you also. Do not try to shape your children's lives into what you think your children should be becoming. Give them space and allow them to express themselves. Support them in their unfoldment rather than direct them in their purpose. Stay with the prescribed statements.

> *"You cannot control what happens to you, but you can control your attitude toward what happens to you, and in that, you will be mastering change rather than allowing it to master you."*
>
> — *Brian Tracy*

Supplement 4

ADHERING TO THE FOUR AGREEMENTS—HEART CHAKRA

"Very little is needed to make a happy life; it is all within yourself, in your way of thinking."

— Marcus Aurelius

Memorize The Four Agreements. I highly recommend the book *The Four Agreements* by Don Miguel Ruiz, which goes into them in detail, but here's a list of them, along with some brief notes of my own.

1) Be Impeccable with Your Word

Be honest and truthful, be authentic, be real, be loving, be kind, but I will add, stay in the moment, react to others from a place of nowness, without influence of history or rumor or labels. Also, speak not of that which is not your business. If it doesn't directly affect you or have something to do with you, leave it alone. No gossiping or spreading rumors—no complaining. No signing of online petitions to persecute people.

2) Don't Take Things Personally

This agreement is critical to understand. What others do is about them, not you. What another person says about you is about that person, not you. What another person says about anything, or does, is about the other person; his or her actions are a reflection of that person and his or her dream of reality. So when someone tells you something about you, understand that. Don't take it personally because what people say is much more about themselves than you. You need to tune into who you are and become secure in yourself, regardless of what anyone says to you. There is an energy to life. Learn to embrace it and flow with it rather than resist it—become who you are, not someone you're being told to become. Don't allow your flow to be forced by others.

3) Don't Make Assumptions

Just as you don't take things personally, you cannot assume you know anything about anyone else. In so doing, if you do make assumptions, you reflect your dream of reality about them. Just as you do not want others to make assumptions about you, you should not make them about others. You never know what is the whole picture in regards to someone else's life. You have no idea what someone else may have suffered or endured. Don't worry about other people. It's none of your business anyway! Be the best you can be! Focusing on your own business and allowing others to be who they choose to be without your judgment or assumption is key to your happiness and to world peace. Never assume, for example, that someone does not like you. Never assume someone is mad at you. Never assume someone has neglected you or some task on purpose. Also, never assume you know anything about another person, unless that person has directly told you or you personally observed it.

As Don Miguel Ruiz says, "This one Agreement can change your life."

Every child of an alcoholic thinks he or she is the reason Mom or Dad drinks. This is just one example of an infinite list of assumptions we make about other people. Rather than making assumptions, talk, if not to that person, to someone else. Work out how to let go of the assumption; clear the air. Make it a priority to learn how to let the need to make assumptions go. When we learn to let go of our knee-jerk way of responding and learn instead to live from the moment, we totally shift the energy and frequency around us and we get into the flow.

It can be extremely difficult to overcome our programming. Being in the hospitality industry is a good example. You meet a wide variety of people, and it is true that there are certain kinds of reservations, or cultures, or addresses, or appearances that will trigger a knee-jerk response.

To be mindful is to learn how to meet each person as if he or she has no history, without any prejudice or assumption. That new person is not related to the other "problem" customers. While people may share certain characteristics, whether it be race, nationality, or address, for example, each human is an individual expression of the Divine, of the All That IS, of the Whole, and deserves a non-prejudiced respect. How lucky if you happen to be working in an industry that blesses you with such a great mindfulness training ground! Any service industry offers great practice for learning to see each person as unique and valuable. To be a whole, healed human is to love each person who comes before you as yourself.

4) Always Do Your Best

Our natural state is a desire to do our best. We are born with the wiring to do our best—expansion and growth: This is the purpose of life. This will seem like a given to many of you, but for some, it will be a new concept, in all likelihood because your best has been beaten out of you either physically or psychologically or both. Once you have healed, doing your best will come naturally to you again. Anyone who doesn't resonate with doing his or her best will first want to address that issue, and get help to resolve whatever it is that is impeding the desire to do your best. The universe doesn't reside within you to do anything other than be great and help make the whole better.

We are, after all, creation in expression. When you stop and think about it, why would the Creator, our Shared Parent, ever create anything defective or diminished or less than in any way? The Creator doesn't. It is only our third-dimension limitations in understanding and a misunderstanding of appearances that causes us to look upon things and each other as anything other than incredibly beautiful and celestial.

Forgive yourself for forgetting you are the Creator in physical expression, that you are a part of the All That IS, that you are eternal life in physical form. You are capable of amazing and incredible deeds. You need not try to be special; you already are. You need only to be your natural self, to be your best good self.

I most highly recommend *The Four Agreements* by Don Miguel Ruiz. He goes into much more detail on each agreement.

*"Always do your best.
What you plant now, you will harvest later."*

— Og Mandino

Supplement 5

LEARNING TO CONTROL YOUR WORDS — THROAT CHAKRA

"If it's very painful for you to criticize your friends—you're safe in doing it. But if you take the slightest pleasure in it, that's the time to hold your tongue."

— *Alice Miller*

In addition to controlling your thoughts, you need to learn to control your language—not just with others but with yourself. It is often easier to focus on changing our language with others than to turn off the critical self-talk in our heads.

Get rid of all limiting words, such as never, can't, won't, shouldn't, no, maybe, might, could, isn't, ought, etc.—even hope. You might be asking yourself "What's wrong with the word 'hope'?" Hope implies a lack of faith. Hope conveys to everything that you are unsure.

Remember that everything is listening. The tone of your language is critical. The words you use are critical. Thoughts and words are things. They have a vibrational frequency, like everything else. Remember Abracadabra? You create as you speak. Not under certain circumstances, but always!

Remember you are creating; you are a creator. Remember everything is energy; everything has a frequency. You create by working with frequency. You create by speaking. Your thoughts and spoken words are things. They exist, and their energy goes out from you and permeates all that is around you.

> *"You can change your world by changing your words.... Remember, death and life are in the power of the tongue."*
>
> *— Joel Osteen*

What do you want? Rather than complaining or talking about what you don't have, or what you don't want, switch it up. What do you want? Speak about what you want as if you already have it, or you know it to be on the way to you. Know that as you declare to the universe your desires, everything is listening and the entire universe will work to fulfill your desires. Let me say this, however: What you want cannot involve harm to anyone else or be motivated by selfish, mean, or unpleasant desires. You are a part of the whole; therefore, you must stay aware that what you do affects the whole—anything selfish or mean is an attempt to separate yourself from the whole and will not serve you.

What happens to another happens to you. The All That IS will not help you if it means hurting anything else in any way because it is not going to hurt itself.

Words have a frequency, so it's important that you choose a high frequency for yourself and high frequency words, if you want to raise your frequency and energy.

You can refer to page 123 for a review of the "Hawkins Scale of Consciousness" or visit the book website www.WalkingThroughYourWalls.com to see some graphics. The Hawkins Scale is a very useful gauge by which to measure your energetic reading and output.

As you will see on that scale, love is 528 hertz. Fear is down around 100, and Infinite Love is at 700-1,000 hertz. So your language is important. If you are speaking fearfully or in a discouraged or depressed way, you are magnetizing that kind of energy to yourself. If you are speaking lovingly, with faith and purpose, then you are magnetizing this kind of energy to yourself. If you are speaking of things you don't want, you are magnetizing those things to you. Speak always of what you do want.

When you are required to pay more tax, for example, think of it as an opportunity to give to the larger whole rather than feeling resentful that you must pay more. Instead of saying you are paying more tax, say, as my friend Rissie says: "I am giving more back." Put a positive spin on everything.

It's always possible to find a positive or uplifting way to say something. For example, imagine a meditation circle where each participant has lit a candle. When the meditation is over, and we've concluded our meeting, there is a danger of spilling wax if the candles are moved, so we ask: "Please blow your candle out, and leave it where it is." Instead of saying: "Please blow your candle out, but don't move it." It may be subtle, but can you feel the difference energetically?

Watch your words as they leave you; become an observer. Listen to how they fall as you speak them. Unless you are already aware of your words, you'll begin to realize as you listen how just in speaking you are altering the energy of your life—many times with buts and don'ts, and I can'ts.

Speak with faith. Believe in and express your belief in unlimited possibility. Find ways to switch statements from negative energy to positive.

"Speak clearly, if you speak at all;
carve every word before you let it fall."

— Oliver Wendell Holmes, Sr.

Supplement 6

STARTING YOUR DAY WITH A WRITING EXERCISE — THIRD EYE CHAKRA

"Whether you're keeping a journal or writing as a meditation, it's the same thing. What's important is you're having a relationship with your mind."

— Natalie Goldberg

Writing in a journal is an extremely powerful tool. An even more powerful and often overlooked tool is to be purposeful in your writing, rather than just writing your thoughts, as many think when they hear "journal."

Writing by hand is a powerful connection to your brain and all the cells of your body. There is a secret to handwriting; in The Tools section in Volume II, we'll talk about the power of handwriting in more depth, including how to make your handwriting powerful through the focus of your handwritten strokes.

In the meantime, it's well-proven that children benefit when they write by hand, and a study in the *Journal of Cognitive Neuroscience* shows that adults learning a new language remember its characters better if they write them out by hand than if they produce them with a keyboard. It's my personal theory that this one tool of repetitive writing can do wonders to shift the energy of your life. It is a really good way to start your journey, and an excellent habit to start your day with.

By writing the same thing each morning, you are reprogramming your subconscious; repetitive writing is one of the most powerful, reliable, and fastest ways to reprogram your subconscious and conscious mind. Why do you think teachers used to make students write some phrase on the blackboard 100 times? Do you remember that? "I am quiet and keep my hands to myself." Or "I listen to the teacher, and I am respectful." Or "I am kind to the other kids and treat everyone as I would like to be treated." Some teachers, who didn't quite understand how life works, would have kids write things in the negative—"I will not talk in class," for example—but they were still trying to employ the same reprogramming principle.

I spend as much as two hours in the morning focused on repetitive writing. It becomes a form of meditation. Over the years, the text I have written has changed significantly, but the purpose has always been the same: to become the best me I can be, to become the me I came here to be, to be the me I was sent here to be, to fulfill my life purpose, whatever good that may be. I use journals stamped with Mahatma Gandhi's quote: "Be the change you want to see in the world."

I can tell you that if you make it your mission to be the best you that you can be, you will never go wrong.

I write out a combination of several select pieces, which I will share with you here and also list independently in the Appendix.

"The Credo" has become my favorite writing. I like the Credo because it really covers you from head to toe, inside and out, and takes long enough (about forty-five minutes) to write out that it gets your focus for a sustained time. I also write out the Unite Invocation and the Eight Intentions that make up WE LOVE US. These two latter pieces are great if you only have a few minutes to dedicate. You can alternate them, one each day, if you are limited on time. You can start with the time you have, even if only five minutes, but the longer you spend, the faster you will see results.

If you take up this practice of ritual writing and it becomes an integral part of the start of your day, you will feel a difference. You will see a difference. Life will start to get easier—magic will show up.

"I have always been delighted at the prospect of a new day, a fresh try, one more start, with perhaps a bit of magic waiting somewhere behind the morning."

— J.B. Priestley

I believe in taking control of life, and a good way to start is developing a ritual for your morning. By establishing a ritual for your morning, you can help start the day on the right foot. If you already have a practice of yoga or another mindfulness practice and you can integrate some repetitive writing into it, you will significantly augment your routine.

I have been using the technique of writing something that reflects my intentions each morning for years and years. In 2015, I adopted the habit of writing out the credo below, taken from Chapter XII of *The Life & Teaching of The Masters of the Far East, Vol. 5* by Baird T. Spaulding.

The version below is my adapted, religiously neutral version of the Credo, in keeping with the writings of this handbook. In Appendix A, I have this version again and also the original version.

Although there is some dispute as to whether the works of Baird T. Spaulding are the journals of authentic trips to the Far East, there is no dispute that the content of his writings contain great wisdom and powerful teachings.

I have found this piece of writing to be an incredibly powerful tool when written repetitively. When I discovered this credo, I knew immediately how powerful it is. Since I have adopted it, I have noticed a huge change in my physical condition. I feel better physically as I write this than I did when I was twenty years old!

> **Credo**
>
> The Goal is to become one with All That IS. You can start your day as All That IS by taking your first thought of AAH within your own form. Let me say that the Goal is established and always has been established. You are eternal life. The Heavenly Image, AAH, the Oneness of All That IS. Oneness men. Oneness women.
>
> Let me also state that there is no thing or no one to compel you to think of these things. It must be a free will offering of your All That IS self:

AAH I Am united with universal life and power and all of this strength is focused in my entire nature, making me so positive with AAH perfect energy that I send it out to every form, and I make it so positive that all may be transformed into harmony and perfection. I know that they are all in accord with infinite life and AAH freedom and peace.

My mind is fully polarized[20] with Infinite Intelligent Wisdom. Every faculty of my entire body finds free expression through my mind and all humanity does express the same.

My heart is filled to overflowing with peace, love, and joy of Oneness. I see in every face that conquering Oneness. My heart is strong with AAH love, and I know that it fills the heart of all humanity. AAH life fully enriches my entire bloodstream and fills my body with the purity of Eternal Life.

AAH is all life. I am inspired with life with every breath and my lungs take in life with every breath and it fills my bloodstream with vitalizing life.

AAH my stomach is the digestive energy of intelligent and almighty life. Every organ of my body is infused with health and harmony, and my entire organism works in complete harmony.

I know that all my organs are infused with AAH intelligence. All are conscious of their duties, and they work together for the health and harmony of my entire being.

---

20 Polarize: to cause (as light waves) to vibrate in a definite pattern, also to concentrate.

AAH I am the energy that fills all space. I am constantly drawing in this energy from all-pervading AAH life. I know that AAH is that all-wise and loving intelligence imparting to me the mighty, eternal life, and I realize the full dominion from AAH, the Indwelling Presence, in my complete body form.

I praise AAH within for the healing perfection of life. All is life, and I allow all life to come into expression.

All That IS says, "My words are Spirit and they are life," and "If a person keep My words they will never see death."

The intelligent All That IS, the Oneness, sends forth abundance of love to the entire universe.

Supreme Mind is everything. I am Supreme Mind!

I Am Supreme Wisdom, Love, and Power. From the very depth of my heart I shout the glad thanksgiving that I Am this sublime and exhaustless Wisdom, and I demand that I draw it to myself and become completely conscious of this ceaseless Wisdom.

Remember that *thoughts and spoken words are things*!

Shout the glad tidings of joy that you are free, completely free from all limiting conditions. Then *know* that you are free and go forth triumphantly free!

I am reborn into the perfect power of the Supreme Mind of All That IS. I Am All That IS.

Let us walk among all people with the full realization that we exist to impart the joyous Light of Love to every soul. This is, in reality, the greatest privilege. For as we radiate that boundless love of Oneness and AAH to every soul, our souls thrill with the Holy Spirit; we also feel the love of AAH for all humanity. To feel and know this is to feel and know the Oneness in all humanity. This endows us with the healing power and wisdom that Yeshua Ben Joseph is endowed with.

The Unite Invocation is one of the other things I write out every morning in my journal. The Great Invocation is a popular and well-known world prayer, but because of my obsession with words and the energy of words and intentions, I was moved to modify the wording to create the twenty-first century model.

The Unite Invocation

From the point of Light within the Mind of Source[21]

Let Light stream forth into the Minds of All.

Let Enlightenment envelop Earth, and be known by Every One!

From the point of Love within the Heart of Source

Let Love stream forth into the Hearts of All

Let Infinite and Unconditional Love Envelop Earth, and be Felt by Every One!

From the center where the Will of the Source is known

Let Our Purpose on Earth stream forth and be known by All

---

21 "Source" can be replaced with: Our Great Parent, Universe, All That IS, AAH, etc.

> Let The Plan of Love and Light envelop Earth and guide Every One!
>
> Let the Plan of Joy and Happiness work out
>
> And Let Love seal the door where all that's contrary dwells.
>
> Let Universal Light, and Love, and Power restore the Plan on Earth
>
> Let there be peace, and love, and the pursuit of happiness for all!
>
> Let there be love for all of US.
>
> For the Greatest Good of All. Amen.

At the end of each morning's writing session, I close with what I call my gratitudes.

I start by writing "Thank you" twenty-one times—seven lines of three. As I write, I am feeling my gratitude for life. I really focus on the feeling of gratitude, and I bring it up so I can actively feel it. My chest will swell with gladness and I have a real physical response.

I go on to write a page or two of thanks, or gratitudes, for everything in my life. I write thanks for my circumstances, for my husband, for my pets, for everyone who loves and supports me, for our customers, for our comfortable home, etc. These writings will vary some depending on how much room I have on a page or how much time I have. If I am pressed for time and only have a few minutes to write, I start with gratitudes. If I have time to write more, then I do, but at a minimum, I start my day by being grateful.

*"Yesterday is gone. Tomorrow has yet to come.
We have only today. Let us begin."*

— Mother Teresa

Supplement 7

INTENDING YOUR LIFE WITH WE LOVE US — CROWN CHAKRA

"Learning lessons is a little like reaching maturity. You're not suddenly more happy, wealthy, or powerful, but you understand the world around you better, and you're at peace with yourself. Learning life's lessons is not about making your life perfect, but about seeing life as it was meant to be."

— Elisabeth Kubler-Ross

One of the basic problems facing humanity is that there is no guideline by which we all live. There are lots of people with ideas on how to make peace, but there is little agreement. There are many organizations pushing an agenda of love, of peace, of unity; the landscape is littered with them, and yet all of these things remain elusive.

"WE LOVE US" is the answer to my prayer, "How do we create a world that works for everyone?" Through months of meditation, it became clear to me that the phrase is an acronym for eight actions that can be taken to fix everything.

Volume III, Section 6, goes into WE LOVE US in greater detail, but for now, the beauty of it is that it is simple to understand and implement, and no one has to give up anything to adhere to the principles of WE LOVE US.

I recommend you memorize the Eight Intentions that make up the acronym WE LOVE US, and live with these intentions to the best of your ability at all times.

The Eight Intentions or Action Statements that make up the acronym WE LOVE US are a rock solid way to live the life you want, to create a place of peace on Earth/Eden/Gaia, and to fulfill your purpose.

Here are the Eight Action Statements or Intentions:

Say "I AM" preceding each statement.

1. Weaving a Fabric of Unity and Peace at Home and Worldwide
2. Embracing Earth as Irreplaceable and All Life With Respect
3. Loving and Forgiving Everyone Unconditionally
4. Offering Openness, Honesty, Truthfulness, and Transparency
5. Volunteering and Serving Others Daily
6. Ensuring Everyone Gets a Voice and Vote

7. **U**niting the Divided with Infinite Love
8. **S**olving our Problems Together in Harmony

Quite simply, if everyone will adopt these Eight Intentions and live each day by these principles, we will all quickly have the life we want.

We will have peace on Earth/Eden/Gaia.

"If you want to be a voice for peace in the world, begin by making peace a permanent condition of your own life."

— Wayne Dyer

Closing Note

ABOUT WALKING THROUGH WALLS

"Our attitude toward others determines their attitude toward us.... When you judge others, you do not define them, you define yourself."

— Earl Nightingale

The first edition of this book will be released amid the sound and fury of the pundits of fear; among the noise and clatter of the chaos of politics; among the most contentious and lie-filled airwaves the country I live in has ever seen. There's never been a more important time to focus on love and truth and living consciously. The world is hanging in the balance.

Remember the lesson from earlier in this volume—that truth is elusive and often presented by people with ulterior motives and personal gain at hand. As Michael S. Tyrrell recaps so well in his book *The Sound of Healing*, in the pursuit of proving evolution and Darwin's theory, Java Man, Peking Man, Nebraska Man, The Pitdown Man, Heidelberg Man, Neanderthal Man, and Cro-Magnon Man all have fabricated or problematic stories. Falsities and manipulations prevail. The same is true with all we have ever been told, it would seem.

Over and over, we see things we have long been told are true being revealed as frauds. More and more, we see that former news reports have been revealed as falsities. People try to cheat others, or spread lies, or make some other personal gain. The recent attack against Planned Parenthood, with forged video footage portraying events and conversations that never took place, is a perfect example. The depth of deception to which unscrupulous people will stoop to persuade people of lies, all to serve their personal or political agenda, has reached new lows in the twenty-first century.

The entire political system of the United States has been hijacked by a handful of billionaires; little, if any of what we see in mainstream media is unfiltered or uncensored, and I don't mean normal censorship meant to protect small children from overhearing dirty words. I mean the purposeful filtering of the truth and the substitution of lies and deception. "Pants on fire" has become a run of the mill accusation in today's political arena. The media in the U.S. declared the "Democratic presumptive winner" the day before five states, including California, the largest population, voted; clearly, a ploy to manipulate voter turnout.

It's hard to find people telling the truth or being honest.

Remember that real truth is only found within. You are here to be the best good thing you can be; turn inward to find your truth.

Please just remember this: Life is about love. To be here, in this physical form, is to be the love of the universe in physical expression; you are creation in a human body.

You didn't come here to be mean and nasty to others; you didn't come here to suffer or be miserable or unhappy; you didn't come here to live in pain or to inflict pain on others! You are the Creator, the All That IS, who has no interest in self-torture, or self-inflicted misery, except and only, when needed as a path to learning.

This is why, when you truly understand who you are, you will become grateful for *everything*, even what appears as pain or suffering. Everything is a result of the divine mind; therefore, everything is divine. Everything. All really is always well. All war, all suffering, all pain, all riots, all murders, all deformities. It's all divine because each moment is an opportunity to acknowledge the divine in the now.

This is the ultimate enlightenment. To be able to say, "Thank you for the experience," regardless of the experience and any level of pain or suffering, is true wisdom, for as we say thank you in the face of the most heinous acts, we learn the strength within—we see the way and help arrives.

"What you resist not only persists, but will grow in size."

— Carl Gustav Jung

The ultimate secret of life is that it is your choice, in each moment, in each second, what your mind will focus upon and what thought you will embrace. Learn to ask to be shown the way to what you want. Focus on what you want, and learn to ask for help. Learn to love that you have a life, that you can be here in this third dimension, learning things, learning how to be the best you that you can be.

By being the best you that you can be, in the end, you discover love is all that matters. Learning to love yourself and learning to love others. Learning to make peace—these are the things you came here for. Everything else is distraction, a distortion, a delusion.

We all came here for love, joy, giving, and helping one another. By appearances, many people are a bit lost. We don't need the fear and loathing, but we are trapped by the fear. It is the thickest of the walls and the lowest of the frequencies.

So as you navigate your day as a member of society, if you have the privilege of being of age so as to have a voice in your government, please take what it says in this handbook seriously. Take your role and contribution to the greater whole seriously: know and vote your heart.

Vote for the people who promise peace because peace is the one thing everyone always agrees they want, and it is the one thing that will begin the healing needed on Earth/Eden/Gaia.

Vote for the candidates who consistently show the world they have a heart and unlimited love for one and all, and who stand for peace and for everyone. Remember the Intentions in WE LOVE US. Vote for the candidates who will bring us these ideals in physical application.

If there are no candidates who fit the criteria, then that truly is a wakeup call!

You must believe in your voice and that your voice makes a difference in these matters. Don't rule out the write-in campaign possibility. The State of Alaska proved a write-in campaign *can* win. Lisa Murkowski won a Federal Senate seat, and that's not an easy name to spell either, which can make a big difference.

Remember, this life, your life, is yours and yours only to shape, no one else's. What you see in the external world you are creating. This is your playground, your classroom, and your opportunity to grow. So walk with yourself gently on the path through your walls, strive to be your best, and have compassion for your experience. It's uniquely yours. Walking through your walls is a process; it will not happen overnight.

"The journey of a thousand miles
begins with a single step."

— Lao Tzu

APPENDICES

Appendix A

DAILY CREDO — ORIGINAL TEXT AND MODIFIED VERSION

Taken from Chapter XII of *The Life & Teaching of The Masters of the Far East, Vol. 5* by Baird T. Spaulding.[22]

Here are two versions. The first, is the original text. The second version is my version substituting neutral words for all religious words.

Although there is some dispute as to whether the works of Baird T. Spaulding are the journals of authentic trips to the Far East, there is no dispute that the content of his writings contain great wisdom.

Credo — Original Version

The Goal is God. You can start your day with God by taking your first thought of God within your own form. Let me say that the Goal is established and always has been established. You are divine. The Divine Image, God, the Christ of God. God men. God women.

Let me also state that there is no thing or no one to compel you to think of these things. It must be a free will offering of your God self:

God I Am united with universal life and power and all of this strength is focused in my entire nature, making

22 Reprinted from pages 147-149 of *LIFE & TEACHING OF THE MASTERS OF THE FAR EAST, VOLUME 5* by Baird T. Spalding ISBN 9780875163673 with permission from DeVorss Publications. www.devorss.com

me so positive with God perfect energy that I send it out to every form, and I make it so positive that all may be transformed into harmony and perfection. I know that they are all in accord with infinite life and God freedom and peace.

My mind is fully polarized with Infinite Intelligent Wisdom. Every faculty of my entire body finds free expression through my mind and all humanity does express the same.

My heart is filled to overflowing with the peace, love, and joy of the conquering Christ.[23] I see in every face that conquering Christ. My heart is strong with God love, and I know that it fills the heart of all humanity. God life fully enriches my entire blood stream and fills my body with the purity of Divine Life.

---

23 The term Conquering Christ can be a term that people struggle with. My interpretation is that what this term means is the essence of what Yeshua Ben Joseph taught. He explained that what he could do, we all can do; he explained that we are a part of the Great Parent. So this term is the embodied understanding of our oneness, and our unlimitedness, of our "Christ-ness within." This essence is in each of us, but we forget when we look at the people around us. We do not see them as humans containing that "Christ." We do not see ourselves as one with them.

I remember years and years ago when I was in my twenties living in New York City, I was studying how to be more loving, and I remember reading a book that suggested looking at the bums on the sidewalks or in the subway stairwells and remembering that, once upon a time, each of those bums was someone's baby.

To see them as tiny babies, newborns, was a great exercise. I learned a lot about myself doing that exercise, as you will too. You'll find you will try to justify your non-loving feelings. In the end, you must become that Conquering Christ, and you must learn to see the same in everyone else. See in everyone the eternal life that exists within yourself. We are all one.

God is all life. I am inspired with life with every breath and my lungs take in life with every breath and it fills my blood stream with vitalizing life.

God my stomach is the digestive energy of intelligent and almighty life. Every organ of my body is infused with health and harmony and my entire organism works in complete harmony.

I know that all my organs are infused with God intelligence. All are conscious of their duties and they work together for the health and harmony of my entire being.

God I am the energy that fills all space. I am constantly drawing in this energy from all-pervading God life. I know that God is that all-wise and loving intelligence imparting to me the mighty God life, and I realize the full dominion from God, the Indwelling Presence in my complete body form.

I praise God within for the healing perfection of life. All is life and I allow all life to come into expression.

The Conquering Christ says, "My words are Spirit and they are life" and "If a man keep My words he will never see death."

The intelligent Christ, the Conquering Christ, sends forth abundance of love to the entire universe.

Supreme Mind is everything. I am Supreme Mind!

I Am Supreme Wisdom, Love, and Power. From the very depth of my heart I shout the glad thanksgiving that I Am this sublime and exhaustless Wisdom and

I demand that I draw it to myself and become completely conscious of this ceaseless Wisdom.

Remember that *thoughts and spoken words are things*!

Shout the glad tidings of joy that you are free, completely free from all limiting conditions. Then *know* that you are free, and go forth triumphantly free!

I am reborn into the perfect power of the Supreme Mind of God. God I Am.

Let us walk among all people with the full realization that we exist to impart the joyous Light of Love to every soul. This is in reality the greatest privilege. For as we radiate that boundless love of God to every soul, our souls thrill with the Holy Spirit; we also feel the love of God for all humanity. To feel and know this is to feel and know the Conquering Christ in all humanity. This endows us with the healing power and wisdom that Jesus is endowed with.

Credo ~ Adapted Version

The Goal is to become one with All That IS. You can start your day as All That IS by taking your first thought of AAH within your own form. Let me say that the Goal is established and always has been established. You are eternal life. The Heavenly Image, AAH, the Oneness of All That IS. Oneness men. Oneness women.

Let me also state that there is no thing or no one to compel you to think of these things. It must be a free will offering of your All That IS self:

AAH I Am united with universal life and power and all of this strength is focused in my entire nature, making me so positive with AAH perfect energy that I send it out to every form, and I make it so positive that all may be transformed into harmony and perfection. I know that they are all in accord with infinite life and AAH freedom and peace.

My mind is fully polarized[24] with Infinite Intelligent Wisdom. Every faculty of my entire body finds free expression through my mind and all humanity does express the same.

My heart is filled to overflowing with peace, love, and joy of Oneness. I see in every face that conquering Oneness. My heart is strong with AAH love, and I know that it fills the heart of all humanity. AAH life fully enriches my entire bloodstream and fills my body with the purity of Eternal Life.

AAH is all life. I am inspired with life with every breath and my lungs take in life with every breath and it fills my bloodstream with vitalizing life.

AAH my stomach is the digestive energy of intelligent and almighty life. Every organ of my body is infused with health and harmony, and my entire organism works in complete harmony.

---

24 Polarize: to cause (as light waves) to vibrate in a definite pattern, also to concentrate.

I know that all my organs are infused with AAH intelligence. All are conscious of their duties, and they work together for the health and harmony of my entire being.

AAH I am the energy that fills all space. I am constantly drawing in this energy from all-pervading AAH life. I know that AAH is that all-wise and loving intelligence imparting to me the mighty, eternal life, and I realize the full dominion from AAH, the Indwelling Presence, in my complete body form.

I praise AAH within for the healing perfection of life. All is life, and I allow all life to come into expression.

All That IS says, "My words are Spirit and they are life," and "If a person keep My words they will never see death."

The intelligent All That IS, the Oneness, sends forth abundance of love to the entire universe.

Supreme Mind is everything. I am Supreme Mind!

I Am Supreme Wisdom, Love, and Power. From the very depth of my heart I shout the glad thanksgiving that I Am this sublime and exhaustless Wisdom, and I demand that I draw it to myself and become completely conscious of this ceaseless Wisdom.

Remember that THOUGHTS AND SPOKEN WORDS ARE THINGS!

Shout the glad tidings of joy that you are free, completely free from all limiting conditions. Then KNOW that you are free and go forth triumphantly free!

I AM REBORN INTO THE PERFECT POWER OF THE SUPREME MIND OF ALL THAT IS. I AM ALL THAT IS.

Let us walk among all people with the full realization that we exist to impart the joyous Light of Love to every soul. This is, in reality, the greatest privilege. For as we radiate that boundless love of Oneness and AAH to every soul, our souls thrill with the Holy Spirit; we also feel the love of AAH for all humanity. To feel and know this is to feel and know the Oneness in all humanity. This endows us with the healing power and wisdom that Yeshua Ben Joseph is endowed with.

Appendix B

UNITE INVOCATION

This is my twenty-first century adaptation of the Great Invocation, a well-known World Prayer.

The Unite Invocation

From the point of Light within the Mind of Source[25]

Let Light stream forth into the Minds of All.

Let Enlightenment envelop Earth, and be known by Every One!

From the point of Love within the Heart of Source

Let Love stream forth into the Hearts of All

Let Infinite and Unconditional Love Envelop Earth, and be Felt by Every One!

From the center where the Will of the Source is known

Let Our Purpose on Earth stream forth and be known by All

Let The Plan of Love and Light envelop Earth and guide Every One!

Let the Plan of Joy and Happiness work out

And Let Love seal the door where all that's contrary dwells.

---

25 "Source" can be replaced with: Our Great Parent, Universe, All That IS, AAH, etc.

Let Universal Light, and Love, and Power restore the Plan on Earth

Let there be peace, and love, and the pursuit of happiness for all!

Let there be love for all of US.

For the Greatest Good of All. Amen.

Appendix C

WE LOVE US – EIGHT PLANETARY INTENTIONS

Eight Planetary Intentions to make a World that Works for Everyone

I AM:

- **W**eaving a Fabric of Unity and Peace at Home and Worldwide
- **E**mbracing Earth as Irreplaceable and All Life With Respect
- **L**oving and Forgiving Everyone Unconditionally
- **O**ffering Openness, Honesty, Truthfulness, and Transparency
- **V**olunteering and Serving Others Daily
- **E**nsuring Everyone Gets a Voice and Vote
- **U**niting the Divided with Infinite Love
- **S**olving our Problems Together in Harmony

Appendix D

HANDBOOK WEBSITES

Handbook: WalkingThroughYourWalls.com

Handbook Facebook page: Walking Through Your Walls www.facebook.com/WalkingThroughYourWalls

Author: LyndaLamp.com

Author Facebook page: LAMP in Alaska www.facebook.com/LAMPinAlaska

WE LOVE US: weloveus.global

Love By LIGHT: LoveByLIGHT.world

ANGELS Care Inc.: ANGELSCareInc.org

Appendix E

VOLUME I REFERENCES

Section 1

http://www.greatsite.com/timeline-english-bible-history/#-timeline

https://en.wikipedia.org/wiki/Lists_of_deities

http://www.religioustolerance.org/worldrel.htm

http://www.everystudent.com/features/connecting.html

http://churchrelevance.com/qa-list-of-all-christian-denominations-and-their-beliefs/ (Kent Shaffer 6/22/2012)

https://en.wikipedia.org/wiki/Graphical_timeline_of_the_universe time line for the universe

http://www.bibleanswerstand.org/God.htm

http://listverse.com/2013/04/15/10-mind-blowing-theories-about-the-universe-and-reality/

http://www.smithsonianmag.com/history/ancient-pyramids-around-the-world-10343335/#gHmeydtAeaMKVAY3.99

http://christianity.about.com/od/biblefactsandlists/a/History-Of-The-Bible.htm

http://taxfoundation.org/sites/default/files/docs/fed_individual_rate_history_nominal.pdf

http://www.nytimes.com/2012/01/18/us/politics/for-wealthy-tax-cuts-since-1980s-have-been-gain-gain.html?_r=0

http://m.datesandevents.org/events-timelines/24-timeline-of-war.htm

http://www.datesandevents.org/events-timelines/09-inventions-timeline.htm

http://www.infoplease.com/ipa/A0781458.html

http://www.ancient.eu/timeline/religion/

http://www.letusreason.org/Cult11.htm (religion timeline with questionable dates)

https://en.wikipedia.org/wiki/Timeline_of_Western_philosophers

http://www.newsmax.com/TheWire/most-popular-religions-sects-images/2014/05/01/id/569022/

http://www.infoplease.com/ipa/A0904108.html

http://thoughtsontruth.com/index.shtml

https://whyevolutionistrue.wordpress.com/2010/07/20/why-does-skin-color-vary-among-human-populations/ (The map of skin color distribution)

https://en.wikipedia.org/wiki/Human_skin_color (contains a similar skin color distribution map)

http://lingwhizt.blogspot.com/2008/02/principles-of-historical-language.html and http://bawaal.com/blog/wp-content/uploads/2009/08/1_geno_map.jpg (These sites have nice maps of language distribution)

http://joythruyoga.com/energychakras/quotes-for-the-chakras/

http://www.quotegarden.com/index.html

Section 2:

http://thespiritscience.net/wp-content/uploads/2014/11/1fYGP.jpg This graphic shows the spectrum of energy waves from y-waves to low frequency radio waves, and shows the narrow band of energy that our eyes register.

http://www.cdl.org/articles/what-are-some-common-problems-with-language/ (From The Center for Development and Learning. It lists at least nine different categories of problems with language.)

http://www.linguisticsociety.org/content/does-language-i-speak-influence-way-i-think (This fascinating article by the National Linguistic Society, titled "Does the Language I Speak Influence the Way I Think," asks some important questions.

http://www.thisbuzz.com/wow-the-video-thats-taking-the-internet-by-storm-today-will-leave-you-questioning-everything/ (Prince Ea's video)

ABOUT THE AUTHOR

"The writer must believe what he is doing is the most important thing in the world. And he must hold to this illusion even when he knows it is not true."

— John Steinbeck

A certain vulnerability comes over you when you write. It's an opening up and a pouring out on paper of one's spirit and soul, and once the words are there, on the printed page, there's no going back.

Lynda Lamp was born Lynda Ann Martin and added her husband's name Paquette when they married. Because her initials spell out "Lamp," she has adopted that for her pen name.

Lynda has been writing her entire life, from poems for friends' birthdays, to short stories, to articles under the pen name Lyn Howard back in the 1980s, to blog posts in the 2000s.

Lynda's unique life experience of being born awake gives her an unusual understanding of how life works. She has been gifted with an assignment of sharing her insights, and she has dedicated her life to fulfilling her spirit and soul's purpose by illuminating the way to love and peace so others may find love and peace for themselves, for those around them, and for the World.

Lynda has dedicated her life to learning to walk her talk and to become a living model of what she studies. She has healed numerous things in her body, including her eyesight, gluten intolerance, arthritis, gastro-intestinal problems, nail biting, and many other physical maladies. It is Lynda's intention one day to walk through walls by controlling her energetic body and by raising her vibration. People have done it, and anything anyone else has done, you and she are certainly capable of doing.

All her life, since she could first talk, one of the things Lynda has said is: "I'm going to get it (life) right this time so I don't have to come back here again!" Knowing that we become what we think about most of the time, Lynda figures she has as good a shot as any to get things right; so she will do her best to learn all there is to know about these things, and she will share her knowledge with you.

Lynda is an intuitive, a visionary, and a light worker who has had award-winning careers in professional theatre, technical computer sales, and lodging hospitality, along with numerous sub-careers, including author and wordsmith, professional speaker, photographer, life coach, and heart circle sponsor.

Lynda lives with her husband in Alaska where they operate the award-winning lodging retreat, Angels Rest on Resurrection Bay, LLC. (AngelsRest.com)

You may contact Lynda Lamp with your questions, to share your success stories, or to schedule her for speaking engagements, workshops and coaching sessions by sending her an email at LyndaLamp@LyndaLamp.com or by calling 1-(855) 763-LOVE (5683).

BOOK LYNDA LAMP TO SPEAK AT YOUR NEXT EVENT

When it comes to choosing a professional speaker for our next event, you will find no one more inspiring and no one who will leave your audience or colleagues with a more renewed passion for life than Lynda Lamp.

Whether your audience is 10 or 10,000, in North America or Abroad, Lynda Lamp can deliver a customized message of inspiration for your meeting or conference. Lynda understands your audience is interested in hearing stories of inspiration, and achievement, and how they can be happier and more joyful in their own lives.

As a result, Lynda Lamp's speaking philosophy is to humor, entertain, and inspire your audience with passion and stories proven to help people achieve extraordinary results. If you are looking for a memorable speaker who will leave your audience wanting more, book Lynda Lamp today!

Visit the book website to see a highlight video of Lynda Lamp. Contact her through the website, by email or phone to see whether she is available for your next meeting and to schedule a complementary pre-speech teleconference or Skype session.

LyndaLamp.com

email: **LyndaLamp@LyndaLamp.com**

1-(855) 763-LOVE (5683)